CEDRIC MORRIS
AND LETT HAINES

TEACHING ART AND LIFE

CEDRIC MORRIS AND LETT HAINES

TEACHING ART AND LIFE

Ben Tufnell

With contributions by Nicholas Thornton and
Helen Waters

NORFOLK Museums
& Archaeology Service

AMGUEDDFEYDD AC ORIELAU CENEDLAETHOL CYMRU
NATIONAL MUSEUMS & GALLERIES OF WALES

Llywodraeth Cynulliad Cymru
Welsh Assembly Government
CORFF NODDEDIG | SPONSORED BODY

front cover
Cedric Morris, *The Eggs*, 1944
Tate, London
(no.35)

back cover
Lett Haines, *The Lion Hunt*, 1929
Private collection
(no.63)

frontispiece
Fig. 1. **Cedric Morris and Lett Haines with Rubio the Macaw.**

ISBN 0 903101 69 6

Published by Norfolk Museums & Archaeology Service and National Museums & Galleries of Wales for the exhibition *Cedric Morris and Lett Haines: Teaching, Art and Life*, Norwich Castle Museum & Art Gallery, 21 October 2002 – 5 January 2003 and National Museum & Gallery, Cardiff 25 January – 27 April 2003.
Designed by Gerry Downes
Printed in Great Britain by Reflex Litho Ltd

East Anglia Art Foundation
NORWICH SCHOOL OF ART & DESIGN

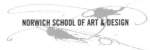

Contents

vi Foreword

1   Introduction
    Ben Tufnell

5   The East Anglian School: 'A common endeavour to produce
    sincere painting'
    Ben Tufnell

23 'The walls of the gallery were splattered with blood':
    The Portraits of Cedric Morris
    Ben Tufnell

31 Cedric Morris and Wales: 'man shall not live by bread alone'
    Helen Waters

39 Lett Haines: The Artist in the Airship
    Nicholas Thornton

47 The Artists
    Cedric Morris 48; Lett Haines 72; Frances Hodgkins 83; Lucy Harwood 86; David Carr 90; Lucian Freud 94;
    Glyn Morgan 100; Maggi Hambling 104

108 List of Works

Foreword

This publication marks what promises to be an important moment in the reassessment of the careers of two major talents of twentieth-century British art. Cedric Morris and particularly Lett Haines have languished unduly in the by-waters of British art, their reputations identified primarily with its ebb rather than its flow. Yet, as the essays of this publication make clear, this is a viewpoint so limited in perspective it is difficult to justify. The impact of their European roots, combined with Morris' strong affinity with Wales, and their joint careers as teachers of art along radical *cours libre* principles has been neglected for too long.

Cedric Morris and Lett Haines: Teaching Art and Life widens our appreciation of the achievement of both artists by showcasing this wider perspective. Works by leading students, notably Lucian Freud and Maggi Hambling, demonstrate the joint achievement and separate inspiration of Cedric and Lett in fostering individuality in their students. The East Anglian School of Painting and Drawing (EASPD), established first in 1937 at The Pound in Dedham, Essex and then at nearby Benton End saw a succession of students, many of whom continue to value the unusual and inspirational environment that the EASPD achieved. Throughout this period Cedric maintained his connection with Wales, teaching miners and establishing institutional support for art and artists in his native land.

The exhibition was initiated by discussions between Andrew Moore and Oliver Fairclough, Keepers of Art at Norwich Castle and the National Museum & Gallery, Cardiff, respectively. Ben Tufnell, Assistant Curator at Tate Britain, is the exhibition guest curator and has organized the exhibition with Nicholas Thornton, Curator of Art at Norwich Castle and Tim Egan, Registrar at Cardiff.

The exhibition would not have been possible without the active help of a number of people. Our thanks go in particular to the lenders who have generously released their paintings. In particular we would also like to express our gratitude to Sir Peter and Lady Wakefield for their support throughout the project, together with Maggi Hambling, and Glyn and Jean Morgan, who have also been active supporters and have given their time generously from the beginning. Richard Morphet (who curated Cedric's retrospective at the Tate Gallery in 1984), and Maggie Thornton and Richard Gault at the Redfern Gallery, have also provided valuable advice. In addition we would like to thank Ronald Blythe, Richard Calvocoressi, Michael Chase, Sally Dummer, Terry Danziger Miles, William Feaver, Anne Lutyens-Humfrey, Andrew Murray, Gwynneth Reynolds and the late Bernard Reynolds, Jenny Robinson, Robert Short, Patricia Scanlan, Hannah Spooner, Katherine Wood, Bod Wright and the staff at the Tate Archive.

Particular thanks go to the Paul Mellon
Centre for Studies in British Art who have
generously funded the publication of this
catalogue. In so doing they have enabled
Ben Tufnell to research the Morris Archive
at Tate Britain and conduct interviews to
bring new information to light. A Jane
Thistlethwaite Travel Bursary, awarded by
the Friends of Norwich Museums,
supported Ben's early work on the EASPD.
Nicholas Thornton has contributed a
perceptive essay on Lett Haines whose
work has too often been overlooked in
histories of British art. Helen Waters, until
recently Assistant Curator (Modern Art) at
the National Museum & Gallery, deftly
highlights Cedric's Welsh roots and lifelong
engagement with Wales. We are also
mindful of the contribution of the art and
exhibition teams at Norwich and Cardiff
who have brought the project to fruition.
We are particularly grateful to the East
Anglia Art Foundation for their crucial
financial contribution, and to Norwich
School of Art & Design for their support of
the project as a mark of partnership
between the School and Norwich Castle
Museum & Art Gallery.

Vanessa Trevelyan
Head of Norfolk Museums & Archaeology

Michael Tooby
*Director, National Museum & Gallery,
Cardiff*

Fig. 2. Cedric Morris in Paris, early 1920s

Introduction

Ben Tufnell

The East Anglian School of Painting and Drawing (EASPD), established in 1937 by Cedric Morris (1889-1982) and Arthur Lett Haines (1894-1978), is one of the most remarkable institutions in twentieth century British art. Away from the metropolitan art world Morris and Lett Haines created a school that was non-prescriptive in the kind of art it encouraged, the methods that it employed, and which inspired an extraordinary level of devotion and loyalty in its students. Many hundreds of students passed through the EASPD, staying for periods ranging from just a few days to many months. A significant number returned year after year across several decades. The school was a place that exemplified a particular *attitude* towards art and life and a vigorous intermingling of the two as much as a place where painting and drawing were taught. It was characterised by a remarkable sense of community which was founded on a love of art, a love of life, and the desire to allow each to enrich the other. At the heart of this stimulating, eccentric and exotic environment were the wildly differing and highly idiosyncratic characters of its two founders.

This publication, and the exhibition it accompanies, explores their work in depth. The selection of Morris' work focuses on his extraordinary flower paintings, perhaps the best known aspect of his oeuvre, and the raw and unsettling portraits which must surely represent his most radical achievement. Helen Waters has written an insightful essay on Morris' deeply felt commitment to his native Wales. A distinguished and inspiring teacher, Lett was an inventive and fascinating artist in his own right. The exhibition includes the first museum survey of his work in almost thirty years and Nicholas Thornton has written the first detailed examination of his art.

Neither this book nor the exhibition can hope to present any kind of definitive account of the School in the space available. In consequence the difficult decision has been made to limit the selection of the students to just five, each representing different periods of the School, and the diversity of approaches which co-existed - a contrast reflected in the work of the two teachers. Many interesting artists have regretfully had to be excluded, including Michael Wishart, Bernard Reynolds, Joan Warburton and Esther Grainger.[1]

Morris and Lett Haines had an extraordinarily wide range of friends and contacts. Besides the students they were always generous in the support they gave to artists less established than themselves. By including Frances Hodgkins we have purposefully widened the scope of the exhibition to take account of the many friends and associates who received their active help. Other artists who received this kind of support and encouragement, and who might have been included in the show, include Christopher Wood, John Banting and Kathleen Hale.[2] Wood for example was elected to the 7&5 Society, then the most advanced artists group in England, at the same meeting as Morris in 1926. He valued his opinion very highly indeed, and in 1928 wrote from Brittany strongly urging him to visit Tooth's Gallery in London and to give him a criticism of his new paintings. He apparently even contemplated moving to Suffolk to live with Morris, whom he clearly regarded as a mentor. Lett wrote that 'Kit was devoted to Cedric & wanted v. much to come and live with us at Higham but Cedric in his innocence, ignorance & prejudice wrote him he could only come & live with us if he gave up drugs'[3]. He went to stay with Ben and Winifred Nicholson instead. Cedric's influence on Wood is very apparent, particularly in his Breton paintings. Indeed it was Morris' trip to Brittany in 1927, and the paintings that he brought back, that inspired Wood to visit there and paint many of his best-known and best-loved pictures.

Both this publication and the exhibition aim to demonstrate the richness of the work of the School, which has in the past been dismissed as a kind of regional oddity, a 'glorified summer school'[4], somehow lacking in seriousness. This is plainly incorrect. In its contemporary context the EASPD represented a radical position. If the teaching at the school could be broadly characterised as following *cours libre* principles, the underlying philosophy of the school – in life as in art – was one of freedom from dogma in every sense.

Notes

1. Michael Wishart was a student 1949-50, and married fellow student Anne Dunn in 1950. Bernard Reynolds was student from 1945, and married fellow student Gwyneth Griffiths, in 1950. Joan Warburton was student 1937-40. Esther Grainger taught with Cedric in Wales and attended Benton End from 1947.

2. John Banting was close to Cedric and Lett in Paris in the 20s (and Cedric painted his portrait during a visit to Céret in 1923) and was a frequent visitor to The Pound and Benton End. Banting's art, which later embraced Surrealist tendencies, is closer to Lett's than to Cedric's. Kathleen Hale, the creator of Orlando the Marmalade Cat, had known Cedric and Lett in Paris and London in the 20s, and moved to Suffolk at the same time as them. She was Lett's lover, and was closely involved with Benton End through to the 60s, often maintaining a room at the house. See James Beechey 'The "magic world" of Cedric Morris & Lett Haines' in *Kathleen Hale*, exh. cat., Michael Parkin Fine Art/Redfern Gallery, London 2001. It should also be pointed out that Cedric was one of a circle of artist-plantsmen, based mainly in Suffolk, which included John Nash, John Aldridge, Rowland Suddaby, John Morley and others. This also lies beyond the scope of the present exhibition and publication.

3. Lett, draft letter to John Allen, TGA 8317.1.1.23

4. William Feaver *Lucian Freud*, exh. cat., Tate Britain 2002 p.17

Fig.3. Left to right: David Kentish, Lucian Freud and David Carr, c. 1939

The East Anglian School: 'A common endeavour to produce sincere painting'

Ben Tufnell

Early Years

In order to understand the endeavour embodied by the EASPD it is necessary to sketch in the events that led to its establishment, and trace Cedric and Lett's movements from Cornwall in 1919 through to their eventual settling in Suffolk at the beginning of the 1930s. Their experiences in Cornwall, Paris (in particular) and London coloured their attitudes towards art, the role of art in life and the teaching of art. This is itself an extraordinary story and we must hope that one day someone attempts what would surely be, given the range of people they knew, a remarkable biography. There is certainly no shortage of material: the Morris archive at Tate Britain contains almost 5,000 items of correspondence and papers relating to the School, as well as Lett's diaries and notebooks.[1] However, for the present publication we must restrict ourselves to tracing their movements and the development of their ideas about art. Those in search of a more detailed biographical account are referred to Richard Morphet's excellent catalogue for Cedric's 1984 retrospective at the Tate Gallery[2].

Cedric Morris was born in South Wales in 1889. He had a number of jobs, including as a farm hand in Canada, before spending a brief period studying singing at the Royal College of Music. A very brief period in Paris in 1914 studying art was curtailed by the outbreak of war and he spent the First World War in the Artist's Rifles, training remounts with AJ Munnings. He was discharged in 1917 and went to Zennor in Cornwall. It was here that he first met Frances Hodgkins, painting a watercolour portrait of her which is now in the Tate. He was in London on (or just after) Armistice Day in 1918, and it is then that he met Lett. Arthur Lett-Haines (known always as Lett) was born in 1894 in London, and was married when he met Cedric. He had served in the army during the War, and was already involved in the art world, having had some formal training 'in Chelsea.'[3]

They were wildly different characters. Glyn Morgan later wrote that they were 'so different in temperament that it seemed impossible that they should live in the same building....'[4] Joan Warburton characterised them thus: 'Cedric and Lett were opposites: Cedric was always himself,

5

instinctive and relaxed; Lett was highly sophisticated and intellectual, he did not curb his non-conformity and he could see through people's pretensions and weaknesses. He was a very good draughtsman and had a splendidly authoritative voice that he used to advantage with his very original wit, sometimes to the discomfort of others.'[5] Christopher Neve illustrated their differences in later life by observing that 'Morris would get up at 6am to weed his iris beds, and Haines got up and had a cocktail in a darkened room at noon.'[6]

Lett, as artist and otherwise, was totally engaged in the contemporary. In contrast to Cedric, who loved nature, professed to enjoy the company of birds and animals above humans, and who displayed a 'creature-like satisfaction with present time'[7] (and consequently abhorred the idea of biography[8]), Lett was at home in the art world. It was his networking and organisational skills that made the EASPD such a success some 20 years later. He kept up to date with all the latest developments in the avant-garde and this was reflected in his work, which is discussed in detail in Nicholas Thornton's essay. Cedric, on the other hand, after a period of experimentation in the early 20s which saw him tentatively explore organic abstraction and imagery influenced by the metaphysical works of de Chirico, remained somewhat detached from subsequent developments in the avant-garde. By the mid-20s he had established what might be called his mature style,

which was to remain more or less unchanged through to his death. While in later years one can draw his work into periods on the basis of subject matter, in formal terms there is an extraordinary consistency.

Between them they clearly made a formidable social force. Their range of contacts was extraordinary, their parties (which were given wherever they established themselves) legendary, and they feature in a number of memoirs of the period.

Soon after Armistice Day Cedric moved in with the young couple and shortly after that Lett's wife left for America. Soon afterwards Cedric and Lett moved down to Newlyn together. In Newlyn they lived in a number of places before creating a large house out of a row of cottages overlooking the harbour, which they called The Bowgie, and which Frances Hodgkins described as a 'Futuristic abode.'[9] Cedric began to make his first oil paintings (see *Landscape at Newlyn* 1919, no.3), which are notable for their tendency to simplify and reduce the motif to a series of flat planes. In Newlyn their social circle included Ernest and Dod Proctor, Laura Knight and Mary Jewels (néeTregurtha), Wyndham Lewis, Edward Wadsworth, Augustus John, and Frank Dobson and his wife Dorelia (whose portrait Cedric painted); they were all visitors to the Bowgie. Nonetheless over Christmas 1920 they sold up and moved to Paris.

During his brief sojourn in France in 1914 Cedric had enrolled at the Académie Delacluse in Rue Notre Dame des Champs in Montparnasse. Now 'the Life Room at the Academie Delacuse which had fallen into disuse became (his) studio and as such was a meeting place for many of his contemporaries. Ford Madox Ford, Juan Gris, Fernand Léger, Hemingway, Ossip Zadkine, Ezra Pound and the Little Review ensemble were particularly intimate and many gay parties of the period were enacted there.'[10] As well as those listed above Cedric and Lett knew Marcel Duchamp, Man Ray (who photographed Cedric), Peggy Guggenheim, Nancy Cunard, Foujita, Brancusi and many others.

Cedric began attending (it is not clear whether Lett did or not) the Académie Moderne (under Friesz, Lhote and Léger), Académie Suédoise, Académie Colorossi, and Académie La Grande Chaumière. These academies were run on the *cours libre* (literally 'free course' or 'free rein') system. In the late nineteenth century such Parisian academies had taught academic painting in the Salon style, and the masters - figures such as Boucher - were leading exhibitors at the annual Salon. As in England at the time students were expected to learn by copying. However, by the 20s standards and methods had been much relaxed. The master was now only likely to appear in the studio very rarely, and was not then expected to spend much time working with each student. A brief critique was the norm. The student was given no direct instruction as such – they

Cedric Morris, *Café Scene*, 1921 (no 46)

were not given practical instruction in the technicalities of paint application, or design or colour theory, nor were they set exercises or projects. There was no course as such, and no classes, the student simply turned up and set to work. Thus it was perfectly possible to be working at a number of academies simultaneously. A student might paint by day at the Academie Moderne before spending the evening sketching at the Grande Chaumière or the Colorossi. For a student such as Cedric – with an unusual but non-academic facility, a strong sense of individualism, and a horror of discipline and rigidity for its own sake – such a set up was clearly perfect, allowing him to develop on his own terms and to concentrate on those aspects of his practice that really interested him. These experiences were formative and when Lett and Cedric were to set up the EASPD it was *cours libres* principles that they would attempt to apply, allied to a more holistic understanding of the conditions required to foster and nourish creativity.

During this period Lett was engaged in making the large ambitious watercolours such as *Composition* 1922 (no.57, p.80), which clearly demonstrate an awareness of the latest developments, and which show a definite, although not definitive, move towards abstraction. While Lett's work seems relatively resolved at this point Cedric was still experimenting with different styles and it was probably Lett who was the better known and more established artist. It is therefore surprising to see that by 1926, when they moved back to London, having both had shows in New York, Lett began to 'manage' Cedric's career at the expense of his own. This was to be the arrangement for the next fifty years, with Lett subordinating his own work in order to promote and organise that of Cedric, who had no interest in administrative things.

By the mid to late 20s what we might call Cedric's mature style was established and his career began to take off with a series of critically acclaimed and commercially successful exhibitions. Frances Hodgkins was able to report of his show at Arthur Tooth's in London in 1928 that 'Cedric is on the wings of an incomparable success – selling & selling – over 40 pictures now gone…'[11] By 1930, when he had his second show at Tooth's *The Scotsman* would comment that: 'Cedric Morris has suddenly become "the rage"… unusual range of subject… freshness, originality and innocence of outlook…. There has been no one-man show more important than this of Morris for the last few months, and this is saying much.'[12] He also showed at the Venice Biennale in 1928 and 1932 and the Carnegie International in Pittsburgh in 1931 and in Pittsburgh and Baltimore in 1934. In addition he was elected to the 7&5 alongside Christopher Wood in 1926 (proposed by Winifred Nicholson, and seconded by Ben Nicholson), and showed regularly with the group until 1932.[13] Such successes would create a set of problems that would eventually lead to he and Lett leaving London, and setting up the EASPD.

Increased visibility meant a greater demand for pictures to exhibit. There was too a demand for pictures of a particular kind: those that would sell (for Morris this specifically meant flower paintings, the only aspect of his work which is completely absent from the substantial group of pictures left in his Estate at his death). Such developments (and perhaps too a lack of serious criticism – see the pointed condemnation in the first EASPD prospectus of 'the system of trading and insincerity of criticism'[14]) led to an increasing feeling of dissatisfaction with the commercial art world and in early 1929 Cedric and Lett took up the lease on Pound Farm, outside Higham in Suffolk. It was to be the first stage in a strategic withdrawal from the metropolitan art world. In February 1930 they gave up their studio in Great Ormond Street and moved out of London. In the summer of 1930 Cedric broke his contract with Tooths, leaving him without a gallery or dealer. In 1932 he resigned from the 7&5 Society and in 1933 he resigned from the London Artists Association.

The Pound was a large, long, old house. 'Its garden was a paradise… you approached it down a tunnel of trees to come out into sunlight. A large black marble torso by John Skeaping graced the forecourt, by a wall was a small greenhouse where Cedric grew cacti and geraniums. Set in the Suffolk pink plaster of this old house were abstract heads and faces by Lett. At the back of the house, which faced south, lay the garden that ran down a slope to a pond. In the middle of this stood a smaller torso by John Skeaping, and beyond was a marvellous view of the Stour valley. The garden was a series of low hedged beds and Cedric's studio, the old wash house, was beside the house in the garden.'[15]

As well as the many house-guests and visitors (and later, students), there was also a veritable menagerie: 'Ptolemy the peacock who strutted about the garden and on the low walls trailing his long tail, Cockey the yellow-crested cockatoo, Rubio the scarlet, green and blue macaw, and ducks – Muscovy and mallard. There were tree frogs in the catalpa tree but they did not survive the winters. The parrots flew about the garden, swung on branches and stumped in and out of the house.'[16]

The Pound was to be Cedric's and Lett's base for the next ten years, and it was there in 1937 that they established the first incarnation of the EASPD.[17]

The East Anglian School: Teaching Art (and Life)

It is not clear how much advance planning went into the School. The first mention in Lett's diaries is on 22 February 1937, just two months prior to the opening, when he notes that he has drafted an advert. Nonetheless, The East Anglian School of Painting and Drawing opened in Dedham on 12 April 1937 (for three days a week initially) with Cedric as Principal and Lett as de facto Director (often referred to in correspondence as the 'secretary' or

Fig. 4. The Pound with sculpture by John Skeaping in the foreground.

'organiser'). Ian Brinkworth was the third member of the teaching staff. While Cedric's name featured prominently on the publicity material, the School was run by Lett. Cedric's involvement with the practical side of the project was minimal, at best. The Pound itself was not used for teaching, although students painted and drew in the garden. The main studio buildings were in the village. Fees were 26gns a year, 12gns a quarter, 5 gns a month, and 2gns a week for periods less than one month, and accommodation was to be found locally. Lucian Freud for example, who enrolled in the early summer of 1939, stayed at the nearby Marlborough Head pub. The School, which was advertised in *The Studio* and *Artist* magazine, was an instant success, and by the close of the first season, in December, 60 students had attended. They held an exhibition of work from the first six months (340 paintings and drawings by 45 students) and the art critic of the local paper noted that 'mastery of technique is often uncertain, but that is to be expected... the whole exhibition showed a lively apprehension of form and colour and an *individuality of approach unusual in the work of students*' (my italics).[18]

Why then was the EASPD so successful in fostering such individuality? The answer is that while it took a progressive approach to art education, it was actually about much more than the teaching of painting and drawing. Esther Grainger wrote that the School was 'The one place where painting mattered; where almost everything else was a joke. A school for more than painting; a world, a sort of family, created, warmed and lit by Cedric and Lett.'[19] At the Pound, as in Newlyn and London, they created what might be termed an *environment*. The prospectus for the School offered 'Instruction in the new forms and their recent development' before outlining the teaching philosophy: 'The object of the school is to provide an environment where students can work together with more experienced artists in a common endeavour to produce sincere painting. We want ...to provide the student with a place where he can work in freedom with every opportunity and encouragement to find his particular form of expression and incidentally to give him an opportunity of creating the atmosphere of enthusiasm and enjoyment which wc feel is essential to the development of his perceptions and the production of good work. We do not believe that there are "artists" and "students": there are degrees of proficiency.... The attitude of the student should be that he believes himself to have a clear idea of creative work and requires help only in its production.'[20]

It is clear then that Cedric and Lett placed context at the heart of their approach to teaching art. In fact, while there was 'teaching' - painting classes, life classes, design classes – the emphasis was rather on the creation of the right conditions in which the student might flourish and develop, *if* they had ability, the right attitude, and were willing to apply themselves.

Fig.5. Students painting by the River Stour, 1937. Cedric Morris is seated on the upturned boat.

Thus the School and its ethos extended beyond the classroom and the studio, into the garden and to the dinner table. This was a world characterised by a vivacious intermingling of art and life, revolving around the creative poles of art, literature (many writers were visitors, including Rosamund Lehmann (no.21) and Antonia White (no.28, p.66), good food, and lively conversation. In the England of the 30s it was exotic and, to a certain extent, suspect. Benton End, where they lived after The Pound, was known locally as 'The Artists' House' and Ronald Blythe has recalled that 'there was a whiff garlic and wine in the air. The atmosphere was well out of this world so far as I had previously witnessed and tasted it. It was robust and coarse, and exquisite and tentative all at once. Rough and ready and fine mannered. Also faintly dangerous.'[21]

In a sense the real achievement of Cedric and Lett's collaboration lies in the creation of this succession of immensely stimulating environments. For some of the students and visitors it could seem like a blast of fresh air. Glyn Morgan, also writing of Benton End, has stressed that at the School life seemed to be lived more intensely than elsewhere: 'I, like many others, began to feel that the creaking old house and the glorious garden were the only real life and the outside world was a sort of shadow-land.'[22]

The first prospectus goes on to reject the idea 'current in the schools that the student is a depository for the theories of the master' and to stress that those who do not have ambition to be professional artists are welcome. 'We hope that this scheme may help, in however small a way, to decrease the division that has grown up between the creative artist and the general public, due largely to the system of trading and insincerity of criticism.'

This encouragement of amateurs, as well as those with professional ambitions, was certainly an important part of the philosophy of the School, and extended to running open classes on Saturdays for locals, which were very well attended. A number of locals went on to make careers as artists – Lucy Harwood and Maggi Hambling in particular exemplify this.

On 26 July 1939, two years after it had opened, the School burnt down. As well as paperwork, artworks by John Skeaping, Frank Dobson, Christopher Wood and Frances Hodgkins, as well as many works by Cedric and Lett, were destroyed. The students painted the gutted buildings (Cedric's version is illustrated, Morphet p.59, Joan Warburton's is in Christchurch Mansion, Ipswich) but there was a serious question as to whether Cedric and Lett would be able to carry on with the School, and if so in what form. They temporarily used the bus garage in the village as a studio (see fig.3.), and also the billiard room at the Marlborough Head. However, by the end of 1939 they had found and bought Benton End, a large sixteenth century house overlooking the River Brett, on the edge of nearby Hadleigh. They originally intended to use it purely as school premises but in 1940 they moved there. This was to be the last, but also the most fully formed and well established of their creative environments, and the name 'Benton End' has now become synonymous with the EASPD and the students who worked there.

'The property, on the edge of the village and overlooking the Brett valley, had been unoccupied for 15 years and what had once been a garden was lost beneath elderberry and brambles. The house with its gables and Elizabethan brick buttresses, was big enough for Morris, Lett Haines and his wife, up to seven or eight living-in students and an equal number of day students who would live in the village. A large studio could be made upstairs, and there was room in the stables for Morris to have a separate studio of his own. The house, outbuildings and about three and a half acres cost £1,000.'[23]

Benton End attracted an unusual mix of students and visitors, and the School was often oversubscribed, particularly during the war. As many as fifteen students lived at Benton End, with others lodging in the village, or with local students such as Lucy Harwood. The School ran from April to October. Students painted indoors and outdoors, both singly and in groups. 'There were life classes with models who came down from London and stayed in the village'. In warm weather these were sometimes held outside (see the photograph in *tate magazine* 29, Summer

2002, p.i). Students were shown how to stretch and prepare canvases and were 'urged to go out into the countryside and by the river'[24] They also made field trips locally to places such as Walberswick. Every day there would be a large and long lunch at 2.30pm, prepared by Lett. Then more painting in the afternoon, with a possible tea break, and a larger and longer dinner in the evening.

Crucial to the success of Cedric and Lett's approach was the social life of the School, and in particular the lunches and dinners, which provided opportunities for lively discussions about art, as well as story-telling and gossip. Indeed, given the way in which memoirs of Benton End dwell on the evening meals – on Lett's extraordinary cooking, which must have seemed incredibly exotic to English palettes used to rationing, employing garlic, herbs and 'exotic' vegetables such as courgettes and peppers, all grown in the gardens and greenhouses – it seems that to many this was almost the most important of the learning experiences on offer. Maggi Hambling certainly thought so. She helped Lett in the kitchen in the 60s and has said that this is where she learnt some of her most important lessons about art. This aspect of life at Benton End must also have made it a tremendously fun place to visit and surely was one of the factors that encouraged students to return again and again.

Lett's cooking was undoubtedly extraordinary given the context of the time.

A group of his menus (and some original recipes), from the early 50s have survived and contain delicacies such as Greek Olives with Smoked Eels on Croutons, *Soupe à Volaille*, Braised stuffed Turbot, stuffed sweet peppers, *Gigot d'Agneau* with Guava Jelly, *macaroni aux legumes*, and selections of French cheeses. Lett and Cedric were good friends of Elizabeth David, who owned *The Eggs*, (no.35, p.57) . She has vividly evoked English attitudes towards cooking at this time; writing about the genesis of her first book, *Mediterranean Cooking*, which she began in 1947, she said: 'I started to work out an agonised craving for the sun and a furious revolt against that terrible, cheerless, heartless food by writing down descriptions of Mediterranean and Middle Eastern cooking. Even to write words like apricot, olives and butter, rice and lemons, oil and almonds, produced assuagement. Later I came to realise that in the England of 1947, those were dirty words I was putting down.'[25]

Given this context a work such as Cedric's *Ratatouille* 1954 (no.40, p.57) appears almost as a manifesto. Glyn Morgan remembered that 'the food when it came was a revelation. I had never tasted such food, I had never imagined that food could be like that....'[26] It has been suggested that cooking became Lett's primary creative outlet once the administration of the School began to prevent him from spending as much time on his own work as he would have liked.

The School was unusual in other ways. Two factors worth noting were the efforts made to promote the work of the students (and to provide extra income), and the absolute equality with which women were treated.

Women attending the School could expect to be treated in exactly the same way as the men, and there was almost certainly a much higher percentage of women at the School than at state art schools. Maggi Hambling has said 'It was never seen as any kind of disadvantage if one happened to be a woman... Prunella Clough, Louise Hutchison, Lucy Harwood... it was to do with freedom and openness of everything, and encouragement....'[27]

As well as holding regular exhibitions of work by the pupils at local venues Lett was also very good at securing commissions for textile designs. Companies who used designs from the students included Caple Silks, Tom Heron's Cresta Silks and Walton's Textiles (Allan Walton was a regular visitor to The Pound and Benton End). Another sideline was the production of pub signs. For example in the late 30s Cedric painted a sign for The Black Horse in Stratford St Mary, Ralph Banbury made one for the Duke of Marlborough, and Joy Collier did one for The Sun Inn, Dedham. This was to develop into a (semi) lucrative sideline for Lett. In his diary for 1948 he notes 'Work on pub signs. Shoulder of Mutton, The Sun (Dedham) + Skinner's Arms (Manningtree).' On 18 September he gleefully notes 'Order for "Bristol Arms" Shotley from Cobbolds'.[28]

A note on gardening

At the Pound and then at Benton End an important part of the environment was the garden. Cedric's gardening activities are beyond the scope of the present essay and those seeking a fuller account are referred to recent essays by Beth Chatto and Ursula Buchan.[29] Cedric achieved international fame in the 50s and 60s as a plantsman as his reputation within the art world began to diminish with reduced visibility. After his Guggenheim Jeune show in 1938 he had solo shows just twice more in London over the next thirty years, in 1940 at the Fine Art Society and in 1952 at the Leicester Galleries, although works continued to appear in group shows at the Leicester Galleries and at the Redfern Gallery. (Later shows in commercial galleries in London were in 1970, 1975, 1979 and 1981). At both The Pound and Benton End the gardens provided the students with a wealth of subject matter – many classes were held out of doors and flower painting was a major part of most students' activities. This was undoubtedly still the kind of painting for which Cedric was best known, and must therefore have represented a major draw for the school. The gardens also provided food, and introduced a different dimension to the social mix, with visits from gardeners (particularly during the iris season).

However, as Cedric's fame as a gardener grew, Lett found the increasing focus on horticulture frustrating. It was

Fig.6. Benton End

particularly hard for him to bear as he had, to some extent, given up his own artistic career to further Cedric's. Maggi Hambling has recalled that Lett only ventured into the garden 'about once a year... his domain was the house, and Cedric's was the garden.'[30] His attitude towards the visiting gardeners – 'these suspect gardeners' as he called them - whom he regarded as an unwelcome diversion, was one of annoyance. Joan Warburton recalled him raging against 'all these fuckers that come to see the bloody garden.'[31]

The School in Context

It is clear then that the set up at The Pound and then at Benton End was unconventional. An unusually vivacious and stimulating atmosphere allied with a commitment to 'sincere painting' meant that the School presented a radical position in the context of the times. Admittedly, being a fee-paying School Cedric and Lett were free to do as they pleased, not being bound to any curricula, but even so their approach is so far removed from that of the state art schools as to appear to be ahead of or out of step with the times.

Art education in England in the early twentieth century was in a largely moribund state. Most of the schools still followed a rigid system (The Kensington Course) which had been developed 50 years previously, and which was based almost entirely on copying. Students only progressed to the next stage of the course when they had demonstrated sufficient proficiency at a set level. Thus it might be many years before they moved on from copying and working from casts to the life room. There were some isolated examples of more enlightened approaches to teaching. At the RCA Professor Moira was noted for developing a method which was 'one of criticism rather than demonstration'[32] and at the Slade, while Tonks' concern with draughtsmanship was apparent in his programme of copying from the Antique, prints and from life, he saw this discipline as the essential basis for developing an artist's individuality.

After 1915, when the National Competition was abolished, the art schools began to break free of the South Kensington System, helped by enlightened appointments such as that of William Rothenstein at the RCA in 1920 (it is interesting to note that Cedric had a brief and unsatisfactory spell as a teacher at the RCA in the early 50s, complaining that his students and the school were smug and uninspired). Nonetheless by the late 30s, when the EASPD was started, it represented a distinct alternative. As Lett claimed, the School 'was founded on the Parisian theories of Cours Libres that the student should develop his own technique and procedure with only the benefit of encouragement by, and the experience of, instructors: a revolution in Art Schooling at that period in Britain.'[33]

There is no teaching institution in the UK in the 30s and 40s with which one can

16

compare the EASPD. The nearest comparison that may be drawn is perhaps with artist communities, such as that in St Ives in the mid to late 40s, where artists worked together, their sense of purpose strengthened and their work emboldened by a sense of community. Another interesting precursor to the EASPD, although at some distance chronologically, is the Herkomer School, which was established in Bushey in 1888 by Sir Hubert Herkomer. Like the EASPD Herkomer's school was an attempt to create a teaching environment in direct opposition to the standards of the day – the 'South Kensington Schools' system - with which he vigorously disagreed. Herkomer 'made it one of his doctrines that a student needed the support of a master who understood his ability and potential and was able to steer the student away from the pernicious influence of slavish copying of another person's style.'[34] A notable comparison with Benton End was 'the freedom and community spirit' that the school inspired in the students, who all lodged locally in a similar set up to the EASPD. The Herkomer School closed in 1904, when it was taken over by one of the students, Lucy Kemp-Welch and run as the Bushey School of Painting until 1911.

The notion of *cours libre* teaching allied to an environment that was conducive to creative work was most fully realised once the School had moved to Benton End, where the making of art could really overlap with the living of life. Glyn Morgan has observed: 'The Pound had been, for all its visitors, a private home with a school as a separate entity. Now, for the first time Cedric and Lett, the school and the garden were all on the same premises. Perhaps this helps to account for the extraordinary intensity of the Benton End experience, for this was not an ordinary summer school but a separate world…. In this house where painting was not just a pleasant holiday task but a way of life, an enclosed world was hidden in an enchanted garden,… but was nevertheless open to all the intellectual currents of the outside world thanks to Lett's restless and tortuous mind. Though so different in temperament that it seemed impossible that they could live in the same building, Cedric and Lett were firmly united in one thing, their absolute refusal to impose styles or ideas on their pupils. The visitor to this exhibition will look in vain for a 'house style'. Their method, if anything so subtle could be called a method, was to try to help the student along the path which seemed to be the natural one for that particular person using a formidable knowledge of design and colour to strengthen the beginner's footsteps. People working at Benton End for the first time would sometimes begin by putting on their paint in Cedric's distinctive manner (referred to by some as Cedric's 'knitting'), but this seldom lasted long. What was encouraged was a complete disregard for fashionable painting or any sort of pretentiousness.'[35]

Despite often giving completely contrary advice both Lett and Cedric commanded great respect from the pupils for their teaching. This was dispensed in a refreshingly ad hoc fashion. By the late 40s there were no classes, '...you started a picture in the studio or in the garden and after a while Cedric would amble up, his hands earthy, filling a foul old pipe from a battered ivory tobacco box. He never told anyone what technique to use. His criticisms were confined to the colour, balance and other basic formal qualities of the painting, so that while you wondered why you had not seen the solution before, the work remained *your* picture.'[36] Lett was a 'thoughtful, generous, fatherly man, treats all the students as his children, refers to us as "you boys", even though some of us are in our forties. He is an extremely good critic and helpful instructor.'[37]

This points to an interesting aspect of the School, which was that while it was resolutely open to different *kinds* of art there was a definite division between those who might be called 'Cedric pupils' and those who might be called 'Lett pupils'. In the present selection the former might include Lucian Freud, Lucy Harwood and Glyn Morgan, while the latter would include David Carr and Maggi Hambling. Those who were followers of Cedric would generally be painters and would paint in such a way as to foreground careful observation, direct statement, and a preoccupation with aspects of painting such as colour and surface texture. Lett's followers, on the other hand, tended to be more experimental, to be less rigid in the way they worked, and be more willing to push their work in different directions. Maggi Hambling, whose career has embraced both figurative and abstract painting in oil and watercolour, as well as conceptual work, and sculpture in ceramic and bronze, is an exemplar of Lett's approach, which was more open to contemporary developments. She remembers Lett, in the 1960s, travelling to London specifically to see the latest exhibitions (including a trip to see the Marcel Duchamp retrospective at the Tate Gallery).

Later Years

The late 1930s and 1940s were undoubtedly the heyday of the EASPD. After the war the character of art education changed as new grants were introduced. As an unregistered art school, Benton End was not eligible and thus attracted fewer new, young students. The same crowd continued to attend, and it became a place geared more to 'holiday painting', although with the same commitment to serious work. Bernard Reynolds has pointed out that in '...the Benton End set up from 1952 onwards... there were very few residential students, mostly frequent or casual visitors who like to claim their association with the EASPD....'[38] By the 60s Benton End was not really functioning as a 'school' any more, although many former students continued to return year after year. It was, nonetheless, still at the heart of a social milieu.

With the decline of the School's activities Lett was able, once more, to devote more time to his own art, going through what might be called a late-flowering of creativity. He made drawings, paintings and collages, and experimented with what he called '*Petite sculptures* or "Lett's weirdies"'[39] – strange, witty, fragile, sculptures made from rubbish and kitchen scraps including bones and egg-shells. Cedric and Lett were by now living almost independently under the same roof. This had always been the case – they often took holidays separately and both had affairs – but the situation was now more pronounced. A visitor to Benton End in the 70s would first spend time with Cedric downstairs, before going upstairs to see Lett in his room (which was also his studio).

Lett died in 1978. Cedric, who had begun to lose his sight in the mid 70s and had been forced to stop painting in 1975, slowly declined into great old age and died in 1982 at the age of 92, shortly after a group of his works, *Lucian Freud* 1940 (no.31, p.61), *David and Barbara Carr* c.1940 (no.30, p.65), and *Iris Seedlings* 1943 (no.34, p.71), entered the national collection at the Tate Gallery.

Lett and Cedric's contribution to art and art education, both individually and together, was significant in a way that their current status within the history of British art belies. Despite his retrospective at the National Museum of Wales, Cardiff in 1968 and the major show at the Tate in 1984 (which toured to the National Museum of Wales and The Minories, Colchester) Cedric remains a marginal figure, something of an outsider. One feels that he would have approved. Yet at the same time this seems curious given the ascendance in the post-war period of the kind of figurative painting, exemplified by the so-called School of London, of which he might be said to be a forerunner. There is an unfortunate way in which figures like Cedric and Lett, who don't fit convenient historical categories, slowly slip into obscurity. Lett, who was concerned about such things, probably would have been disturbed by this thought. Cedric, who hated biography, would surely not have minded either way. Yet it is surprising that their eccentric but inspiring joint project, the East Anglian School, remains little known beyond Suffolk. It is to be hoped that this exhibition and publication go some small way to redress the balance.

Notes

1. The extensive Cedric Morris archive (ref TGA 8317) is held at the Hyman Kreitman Research Centre at Tate Britain. It is supplemented by Lett's papers, and items from John Morley, Bryan Brooke and Joan Warburton (including her unpublished memoir, *A Painter's Progress*).

2. Richard Morphet, *Cedric Morris*, exh. cat., Tate Gallery 1984

3. Ronald Blythe 'A Tribute' in Minories exh. Cat. 1974

4. Glyn Morgan 'Introduction' in *The Benton End Art Circle* exh.cat., Bury St Edmunds Art Gallery 1986

5. Joan Warburton, *A Painter's Progress: Part of a Life 1920-1987*, unpublished. TGA 968.2.20

6. Christopher Neve 'The Outsider' in *Country Life* 26 April 1984 p.1166

7. Ronald Blythe 'Sir Cedric Morris' in Susan Hill ed. *People, Essays & Poems* Chatto and Windus 1983 p.29

8. Joan Warburton reported that she once came across Cedric tearing up old photographs. He explained 'My life is my own and I'm not leaving anything that could assist any would-be biographer'. Joan Warburton, *op. cit*

9. Frances Hodgkins, letter to her mother dated 15 May 1920. See Linda Gill ed., *The Letters of Frances Hodgkins*, Auckland University Press 1993, p.347

10. Lett, mss draft for Cardiff cat. 1968 TGA 8317.6.3

11. Letter to Dorothy Selby 24 May 1928. See Linda Gill, op cit p.407

12. *The Scotsman* 6 March 1930

13. Other members of the 7&5 included Ivon Hitchens, David Jones, Len Lye, and (later) Henry Moore, Barbara Hepworth and John Piper. The 7&5, which consisted of seven painters and five sculptors was widely considered to be the most advanced artist's group in England at the time. When Cedric joined the emphasis was firmly on the figurative but by 1932, when he resigned, the group had begun to move towards a more radical position, embracing abstraction under the leadership of Ben Nicholson

14. EASPD prospectus, n.d, probably 1937. TGA 8317

15. Joan Warburton, op. cit

16. ibid

17. In 1932 Mrs Vivien Doyle Jones, neighbour and student, died and bequeathed The Pound to Cedric.

18. Quoted in Joan Warburton, op.cit

19. Esther Grainger, quoted in *The Benton End Art Circle* exh. cat., Bury St Edmunds Art Gallery 1986

20. EASPD prospectus, n.d., probably 1937. TGA 8317

21. Ronald Blythe op cit p.26

22. Glyn Morgan unpublished memoir, 1992

23. Christopher Neve & Tony Venison 'A Painter and his Garden: Cedric Morris at Benton End' in *Country Life* 17 May 1979 pp.1532-1535. The reference to Lett's wife is curious, and is either a reference to one of Lett's lovers, or a concession to propriety.

24. Joan Warburton, op.cit

25. Elizabeth David, 'John Wesley's Eye' in *An Omelette and a Glass of Wine*, Penguin, reprinted 1986 p.21

26. Glyn Morgan, unpublished memoir, 1992

27. Maggi Hambling, unpublished interview with the author 30 May 1997

28. Lett's diaries TGA 8317.7.2

29. Beth Chatto, 'Cedric Morris: Artist-Gardener' in *Hortus* No.1 1987 pp.14-20. Ursula Buchan 'Iris and Art' in *The Garden* July 1997 pp.472-475

30. Maggi Hambling, op. cit.

31. Joan Warburton, diary entry, 19 Mar 1973 TGA 968.2

32. 1911 Report on RCA quoted in Christopher Frayling *The Royal College of Art: One Hundred & Fifty Years of Art & Design* Barrie & Jenkins 1987 p.80. Interestingly W Staite Murray, with whom Cedric exhibited in 1924, who taught pottery at the RCA, held the opinion that 'A Zen master teaches by not teaching, at least verbally; he merely demonstrates...', quoted Frayling p.110.

33. Lett Haines *Masters and Pupils*, exh. cat., Westgate House, Long Melford, March 1970, quoted Morphet, 1984 p.95

34. David Setford, 'The Herkomer School' in *Stand to Your Work: Hubert Herkomer and his Students* exh. cat. Watford Museum 1983, pp.4-5

35. Glyn Morgan 'Introduction' in *The Benton End Art Circle* exh. cat., Bury St Edmunds Art Gallery 1986

36. Glyn Morgan, unpublished memoir, 1992

37. Bernard Reynolds, diary entry 15 May 1945 quoted in *The Benton End Circle* , exh. cat.,Bury St. Edmonds Art Gallery 1986

38. Bernard Reynolds, letter to the author 27 November 1997

39. Lett Haines 'Preliminary Note on Exhibitions, 1974', TGA 8317.6.3.3

Fig. 7. Cedric Morris, early 1920s

'The walls of the gallery were splattered with blood': The Portraits of Cedric Morris

Ben Tufnell

A visitor to the Guggenheim Jeune Gallery in London in March 1938 would have been confronted with an unnerving spectacle. For his exhibition there Cedric Morris hung the gallery walls three deep with nearly one hundred portraits, twice as many as were listed in the catalogue. The paintings provoked strong reactions. Peggy Guggenheim recalled that at the private view 'one of the guests... so much disliked the portraits that in order to show his disapproval he started burning the catalogues. Cedric Morris, naturally infuriated, hit (him) and a bloody battle took place. The walls of the gallery were splattered with blood....'

Guggenheim recalled that Morris had not wanted to make a show of the 'beautiful flower pictures for which he was famous.' Instead, the artist had persuaded her to let him show his portraits despite the fact that, like the disruptive private view guest, she believed them to be 'in most cases nearly caricatures, all of them on the unpleasant side.'[1]

I don't believe it was Morris' purpose, in painting portraits such as those of *Lett Haines* (no.2, p.60) or *Paul Odo Cross* (no.11, p.24), both of which were included in the Guggenheim show, to caricature or critique his sitters. They were, after all, his friends and students. Morris, as the critic Eric Newton had it, 'merely states the facts as interest him...' He found Morris' work 'a welcome relief from the flatteries and evasions of ordinary portrait exhibitions.'[2] If we see caricature or critique that is our reading, not necessarily the artist's intention. The uncompromising commitment to painting honestly and directly what is before him, rather than falling into any preconceived manner or method leads us now to believe that Morris was pursuing some ulterior agenda. We are accustomed to flattery in portraiture yet these paintings make no concession to beauty. In this respect Morris' portraits of the 20s and 30s, which were disturbing at the time, remain so even now.

Today Morris is still best known for his 'beautiful flower pictures.' However, it is the portraits which represent his most distinctive and radical achievement. Individually they offer us powerful and convincing statements of personality, and as a body of work they present a sustained and vivid picture of an extraordinary milieu. They were distinct from other work being made in Britain at the time – being closer in sensibility to contemporary developments in France and Germany.

The purpose of this essay then is to offer an argument as to why we should reassess Morris' achievement and admit that if he is not the foremost portraitist working in Britain in the 20s and 30s he is certainly in the front rank. Compared to the painters of Camden Town and Bloomsbury, and the artist who to the general public perhaps best represented 'advanced' painting at this time, Augustus John, Morris' best work appears surprisingly modern - ahead of its time in that it seems to articulate (or at least indicate) the existential condition of the individual. These stark heads, subjected to searching examination, convey a powerful sense of the isolated individual in a way that anticipates developments in the 50s, and works by the so-called School of London. Lucian Freud has recalled that, in comparison to other English portraiture of the 30s and 40s Morris's portraits were often 'revealing in a way that was almost improper'[3], something that could undoubtedly be said of his own work.

Why then, are Morris's portraits so distinctive? The most striking aspect of his work is its direct engagement with the subject, which Richard Morphet has characterised as *scrutiny* and 'the exceptional directness with which he realises the subject and communicates its sheer existence.'[4] We are given a sense that

Cedric Morris, *Paul Odo Cross* 1925 (no. 11)

the artist has gained some kind of insight into the essential nature of his subject. Morris wrote: 'There must always be great understanding between the painter and the thing painted, otherwise there can be no conviction and no truth. This might be called "vision" and reality, as opposed to realism. Reality is knowledge and realism is only the appearance of knowledge...'[5] What he is after then, is a way of representing what he sees, without resorting to fakery or mannerism, and in his best work he achieves it.

The essential characteristic of a Morris portrait, which allows the communication of this 'knowledge' is simplicity: of conception, form and composition.

In his use of simplification (and sometimes exaggeration) of facial features Morris seems on occasion to veer uncomfortably close to caricature[6], but his use of such techniques is always in the service of achieving a direct and intense rendering of the subject rather than for comic or satiric effect. Morris' use of reduction in his work is in part inspired by the pared-down quality of Chinese painting, which he admired. He wrote: 'In an indifferent picture the usual redundancy of non-essentials betrays the poverty of the vision... in the monotype of Chao Meng-Chien (thirteenth century)... no brush stroke could be omitted or one added.'[7] Morris' best paintings have the compelling completeness he describes here – as if the image already existed and the artist has simply revealed it. This is borne out in the way that he painted, as if 'unrolling' the painting, without preliminary drawing. Maggi Hambling described seeing Morris at work on a painting: 'He'd started in the top left hand corner and he'd got about two thirds of the way down, and he was going down to the bottom right corner where he would put his signature...'[8]

In composition too Morris pares away the image, focusing on heads and faces almost to the exclusion of all else. Where background is included it is usually a cursory evocation of a generic space – lines and blocks of colour which might perhaps represent a doorway or window (see the portraits of *Lucian Freud*, no.31, p.61 and *Glyn Morgan*, no.38, p.66). Again, the effect is to intensify the psychological impact of the image, to direct all attention to the features and expression of the subject, as if we are making an examination in close focus beneath a microscope. A secondary effect of this is to isolate the individual – which not only gives an impression of monumentality but also singularity – thus giving us images with a pronounced existential quality.

Morris is often praised for his use of colour.[9] His flower paintings and landscapes demonstrate his skill – and the enduring freshness of his colours – but it is perhaps surprising to note that in his portraits too, colour plays a crucial role. He characteristically places his sitters against a strongly coloured background, which either corresponds with, or complements, the sitters clothing, thus creating a unified

25

composition and intensifying the impact of the image, or which creates a psychological space. For example, *Mary Butts* (no.8, p.62) – a notorious partygoer and heavy drug user – is depicted against a hellish red background. Her orange jumper, golden hair, and the odd greenish tints that light her face, together with the peculiarly transfixed expression on her face, all combine to create a singularly intense image.

Morris' work of this period seems to have more in common with contemporary concerns on the continent than with British art. Morris and Lett Haines had moved to Paris at the end of 1920, and their social circle there included not only such ex-pats as Nina Hamnett and Mary Butts, but also many of the international avant-garde, including Kisling. Morris's use of radical simplification (and distortion) in his work of the 20s leads us inevitably to comparisons with the work of Kisling and more particularly with his friends, Soutine and Modigliani (who died in 1920). Morris would almost certainly have seen portraits by Modigliani, which had been included in a show of French art at the Mansard Gallery in London in the summer of 1919, and which would have been on show at dealers such as Paul Guillaume in Paris when Morris was there. Morris and Modigliani's drawing styles are certainly very close to each other, making telling use of reduction of form and purity of line. Morris' portraits are closest to the least excessively stylised of Modigliani's works,

Fig.8. Amedeo Modigliani, *Potrait of a Girl* c. 1917 (Tate, London)

such as the portrait of *Chaim Soutine* c.1916 (Staatsgalerie, Stuttgart) and the *Portrait of a Girl* c.1917 (Tate, London), which was exhibited at the Lefevre Galleries in London, in March 1929. One could also draw comparisons with other artists working in Paris at this time, particularly those involved with the 'return to order', such as Picasso, Derain and Severini, in their use of clear, simple forms.[10]

Morris and Lett used Paris as a base and travelled widely in Europe in the early 20s. They were in Italy in 1922 – and the influence of the metaphysical painters such as De Chirico briefly manifests itself in works such as *Golden Auntie* 1923 (no.7 p.51) and *Patisseries and Croissant* c.1922 (no.5, p.50) – and in Germany in 1921 and 1922.

Morris was certainly interested in the early German masters such as Cranach and Dürer, but the question of whether or not he was familiar with, and influenced by, the artists of the German Neue Sachlichkeit ('New Objectivity') is more difficult to answer. Painters such as Otto Dix and Christian Schad were not much known in Paris and London at this time. However, it is possible that Morris saw work by these artists when he was in Berlin in 1921 and 1922. It is highly likely that by 1922 he had come across Dix, who had exhibited paintings of prostitutes in Berlin to general outrage and was certainly the best known (or notorious) avant-garde artist in Germany. The hellish reds, pinks

and oranges in Morris' 1924 portrait of *Mary Butts* may recall Dix's celebrated portrait of the journalist Sylvia Von Harden (painted in 1926), however Morris did not subscribe to the kind of ideas that Dix was pursuing, and which were then being characterised as Verism. 'Verism' (or 'verismo' in Italian), was a term first used by a reviewer in the avant-garde periodical *Das Kunstblat* to characterise a style of uncompromising realist painting, somewhat old-masterish in finish. More precisely Paul Ferdinand Schmidt (whom Dix painted) used the term in 1924 to describe a socially critical tendency and 'the pessimistic rejection of the illusion of beauty'[11] in the work of Dix and others. Morris' work certainly rejects the illusion of beauty, but to say that it does so through pessimism and as a means of effecting a social critique would be false.

In Britain Morris was prominent in the art world in the 20s and 30s, although subsequently he has tended to be neglected in accounts of the period. Reviewing the period 1918-38, in 1951, Hesketh Hubbard asserted that 'the outstanding portraits came from John, Orpen, Walter Russell, McEvoy, Connard and Glyn Philpot.'[12] Hubbard is writing of more academic portraiture here, but if we turn to Modernist practice in Britain we find that no other artist was making such a sustained engagement with the genre at that time. Many of Morris' friends and contemporaries – including Wood, Gertler and Roberts – make the occasional portrait, but it cannot be said to represent a central

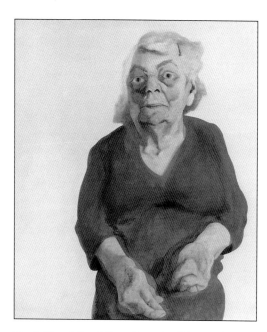

Fig.9. Maggi Hambling, *Portrait of Frances Rose,* 1973 (Tate, London)

part of their practice in the way it does for Morris.

While in a wider context there are strong similarities between Morris' work and that of a number of his contemporaries,[13] in portraiture Morris is a singular case. Not only is his commitment to the genre unusual but his highly personal approach to the problems of painting a convincing depiction of a human being is distinct. While contemporaries as varied as John Banting, Thomas Lowinsky and Stanley Spencer all painted exceptional portraits during this time, Morris still seems to stand apart for the uncompromising intensity of his best work.

In later years Morris' portraits have also been important for his two best-known pupils, both of whom have professed admiration for this aspect of his work above all others. Lucian Freud's early work is much indebted to his teacher, as can be seen particularly in his own portrait of Morris (no.92, p.97) and later works such as his portrait of *John Deakin* 1963-4 -all ears and nose, close cropped, careful scrutiny and focus on the shape of the head and individual features- which also demonstrates a strong concern with surface texture. While Maggi Hambling's exceptionally fluid later style, as seen in her recent portraits of her father, is far removed from that of Morris, her work of the 70s, and in particular her portraits of her neighbour Frances Rose are much indebted to her former teacher, both in terms of composition and in the handling of the paint.

The incidents at Guggenheim Jeune in 1938, and Peggy Guggenheim's comments that the works were unpleasant caricatures, give us a valuable insight into the way that Morris' portraits were viewed (particularly in relation to the flower paintings) at that time by general public, cognoscenti, and the artist himself. Largely they were misunderstood. We should not be so hasty in judgement. These portraits are some of the most remarkable paintings done in Britain in the first half of the twentieth century.

Notes

1. Peggy Guggenheim, *Out of this Century: Confessions of an Art Addict*, Andre Deutsch 1980 pp.171-2. Another account of the opening is in Joan Warburton's unpublished memoir *A Painter's Progress* (TGA 968.2.20): 'I heard later that one sitter who did not consider his portrait flattering was so angry that he took it off the wall and stamped on it.'

2. Eric Newton, 'Uncompromising Portraiture: the temptations of water-colour' in *Sunday Times* 27 Mar 1938

3. Richard Morphet, *Cedric Morris*, exh. cat., Tate Gallery 1984 p 85

4. ibid. p.80. For a discussion of the notion of 'scrutiny' in English art in this period see Richard Morphet 'Realism in English Art, 1919-1939', *Cahiers du Musée National d'Art Moderne*, nos.7/8, 1981, pp. 342 - 345

5. Cedric Morris, 'Concerning Flower Painting', *The Studio* CXXIII May 1942 pp. 121-132

6. For a discussion of caricature in art see E.H. Gombrich, *Art & Illusion*, Phaidon 1960, pp.279-303

7. Cedric Morris, op cit.

8. Maggi Hambling, unpublished interview with the author 30 May 1997

9. Morphet calls him 'one of the most exceptional colourists in twentieth century British art' p.87

10. Elizabeth Cowling and Jennifer Mundy, *On Classic Ground: Picasso, Léger de Chirico and the New Classicism 1910-1930*, exh. cat., Tate Gallery1990. See in particular cats. 48, 152, 156, 160

11.Quoted in Sarah O'Brien Twohig, *Otto Dix*, exh. cat., Tate Gallery 1992, p.108

12. Hesketh Hubbard, *A 100 Years of British Painting 1851-1951*, Longmans 1951 p.267. Surprisingly, the book makes no mention of Morris.

13.See Morphet pp.34-41

Fig.10 Cedric Morris in the studio at Benton End

Cedric Morris and Wales: 'man shall not live by bread alone'

Helen Waters

The place of one's birth holds different significance for different people. Some leave their birthplace when they are too young to remember, never to return or to give it a moment's thought; some spend their whole lives within the boundaries of the same town or village and have no knowledge of or desire for anything else. Others are born and grow up in a particular place which stays with them forever. It doesn't matter whether they travel the globe or where they settle; their first home remains closest to their heart and the place where they feel they truly belong. Cedric Morris was one of those people.

Morris was born in 1889 in Sketty, Swansea in South Wales. His family had settled there many years before; indeed the first baronet, Sir John Morris (1745-1819), who made a fortune from copper and coal, created an industrial suburb in Swansea and endowed it with the family name: Morriston still exists to this day. Cedric grew up in Glamorgan, on the Gower peninsula and his love of the landscape and the people remained with him until he died. Although he was sent to school in England and never settled permanently in

Wales after childhood, as an adult he returned time and time again to the country of his birth and felt a great affinity with it. Perhaps he inherited this sense of patriotism from his father, who represented his country in Rugby as an amateur international (and was even known locally as 'Morris the Football').[1] Certainly, Morris felt that the land was a part of him and his roots. In a letter to Lett from Swansea in July 1928, he wrote, 'I always said this was the most lovely country in the world and it is – its so beautiful that I hardly dare look at it – and I realise now that all my painting is the result of pure nostalgia and nothing else – I thought I was home sick for England but not at all – it was this I wanted and now of course I shan't be able to paint it – there's too much to do – everywhere its paintally (sic) and it all looks like my landscapes only 10 million times better – the colour is marvellous and so is the shape…. perhaps it's because I came out of it… I think Pa must have had some dirt out of the garden on his thing the night he made me – anyway I'm perfectly happy here…'[2]

Wales was more to Morris than a source for his paintings, although the landscape of

Cedric Morris, *Llanmadoc Hill, Gower Peninsula*, 1928 (no. 16)

the valleys did provide him with inspiration for some wonderful works. For Morris, Wales was his home and the home of his people – he felt a duty toward them and throughout his life he returned to the goal of enriching their cultural lives. 'Something is drawing me into the middle of this', he wrote in 1935, from Penclawdd, 'I want to go away but I can't – I feel in a curious way it is part of me that came out of it and that in some way I must go back into it.'[3]

Morris wrote this letter in 1935, a year that was to be significant in the reassertion of a distinctively Welsh cultural identity. This was the year that Morris, with Augustus John, selected and organised (with the support of other affluent and influential Welsh men and women)[4] an exhibition of Welsh contemporary art, which toured the nation and led to the founding of the Contemporary Art Society for Wales.[5] The exhibition opened at the National Library of Wales, Aberystwyth, on 16 July 1935 and toured first to the Francis Davitt Gallery, Swansea (13 September – 3 October) and then to the National Museum of Wales, Cardiff, where it closed at the end of November. In a letter from the exhibition secretary, Mrs Frances Byng-Stamper, it was described as 'the first travelling exhibition of its kind that has ever been organised.' The statement that was issued to publicise the show displayed a passionate sentiment, which reflected the emotive rationale behind the event:

'THE CONTEMPORARY
WELSH ART EXHIBITION

The endeavor of this Exhibition is to bring before the people of Wales the urgent importance of Art in our National development. It has long been apparent that the visual Arts, greatest of all vehicles in the expression of the soul of a nation have suffered damage and deterioration at a period beginning in the middle of last century; and it may be as well to emphasize that Art is the highest manifestation of human activity.

Amid the turbulence caused by the rise and wane of great industries the creative instincts of our people have too often been thrust aside in the struggle for daily bread (but)... it has been written that Man shall not live by bread alone... and it is essential that more of us should take heed for our racial immortality. We believe also that the Welsh, whose artistic perceptions are more lively than those of other nations, should take a definite lead in the cultural renascence of these Islands: we have therefore brought together for exhibition, Paintings and Sculpture of truly contemporary Welshmen at home and abroad: by contemporary is meant that the co-operation has been invited of those best representative of the Welsh Artists whose vision is adequate to their own time and may well add to the tradition of Art and Civilization which is WALES.'[6]

Despite the turbulent times in which it took place, or perhaps because of them, this touring exhibition proved to be extremely popular with the general public. Morris notes in a letter to Lett from Manorbier Castle, the home of Frances Byng-Stamper[7] on 28 July 1935, that 'everything seems to be going well at Aberystwyth. 2000 visitors to the exhibition in one week.'[8] From his letters at the time, we can follow Morris as he toured Wales, often alone, occasionally with John, working tirelessly on the exhibition, as well as visiting political leaders of the area and giving talks on painting to the unemployed miners of the district. Morris was painfully aware of the poverty and the problems that the people were experiencing in the face of mass unemployment and other consequences of the Depression. He writes in great detail with genuine amazement and respect at how the people cope – 'it is really heartbreaking the way they have to live'.[9] Sometimes his despair betrays a pessimism: in another letter to Lett, written 8 August 1935 he writes, 'It is dreadful to think that there is nothing for them – that S.Wales can never recover and that they and their children will all have to die in this disgraceful poverty – so much for industrialisation.'[10] And yet, amidst this negativity, comes an admiration and an optimism: he finishes the same letter by saying, 'there is none of that dead feeling of isolation and indifference and futility here – a childish eagerness to know and understand and to cultivate themselves – of course they never will with all this bad stuff dished up at them, but this enthusiasm is very comforting after England.' Morris had always felt more affinity with Wales than England and often turned his anger at the situation in South Wales against the English. In a particularly bitter letter he writes, 'I don't think I can go on living in England... I am ashamed of being an Englishman and I hate England, but there doesn't seem anywhere else for me to go ... – and now what will happen to Wales? ...I have never in my life felt anything like this...Surely this in the last blot on an infamous history and the sooner this stinking old whore of a country is blown out to sea the better – except that it would dirty the sea. If only there was something one could tie oneself onto that was against all this, but there is nothing – fat complacency everywhere – perhaps a few half-starved, frightened miners who have got to be murdered anyway to make way for more complacency. I don't know what to do for them...'[11]

Cedric Morris, *The Tips, Dowlais 1935* (no. 27)

Morris seemed to feel powerless politically to help his fellow Welshmen and perhaps, because of this, decided to use what he did have to assist them: his purse and his talent. During this time, he would often take lodgings in the homes of out of work miners, who were grateful of the extra income.[12] He also began teaching them. 'I am starting evening classes for various kinds of design and handicraft – 2 nights a week and every afternoon...' , he wrote to Lett from Gwernllwyn House in Dowlais in December 1939, '...We start with wallpaper, some woolworth colours, brushes, pencils and some very good clay off the mountains – they are all young or youngish – I shall stay on some weeks to get this going. I expect you will think it mad and probably there's no talent, but perhaps there is...' He continued with this class for a month and then handed it over. Gwernllwyn House was bought by Miss Mary Horsfall and turned into an educational settlement. These settlements were established across South Wales during the thirties as a way of developing education and a sense of community amongst the growing number of unemployed.[15] Cedric became a trustee of Gwernllwyn House and continued to visit on a regular basis, giving talks and taking classes.

Morris kept up his support of art in South Wales after his initial efforts in the 1930s. In 1946 he became President of the South Wales Art Society. Along with Ceri Richards and David Kighley Baxandall (former Keeper of Art at the National Museum), he was one of the selectors of the first exhibition of the South Wales Group (now known as the Welsh Group). This exhibition opened in the Pyke Thompson Gallery at the National Museum in Cardiff in 1949 and then toured around the country. The show included the work of many friends and students of Morris: Esther Grainger, who was in charge of the teaching at the Pontypridd settlement; Heinz Koppel, whom Morris met through Grainger and who became painting instructor at the Educational Settlement in Merthyr Tydfil; Renate Fishl, one of

Fig. 11. Postcard from Cedric to Lett, from Manorbier, Wales

Cedric's students in East Anglia, who married Koppel; Arthur Giardelli, who taught at Dowlais, and Glyn Morgan, another student of his. By 1955 he had become an artist member himself of this group. The Contemporary Art Society for Wales, which Morris had helped to found back in the 1930s, invited him to be Vice-President in 1967 and he retained that position until 1981, when he was over ninety years of age.

Morris's support of these art organisations, all of which still exist to this day, was reciprocated through their support of him as an artist. His work was bought at regular intervals by the Contemporary Art Society for Wales and redistributed to museums and galleries across the country, and his work was exhibited in Wales throughout his life.[14] During his time teaching or organising exhibitions, Morris never stopped painting himself. Whilst at the Gwernllwyn settlement, he painted the surrounding area in Dowlais – the post office, the tips, the church (nos 26 and 27). The landscape of Wales provided him with endless subject matter, which he often found overwhelming: in 1933 he wrote from Scotland House, Solva, 'I have never seen Wales so lovely…it makes me quite dizzy.' Around the same time he painted a wonderful canvas of the town (no.23, p.54), which seems to demonstrate, simply, but effectively, the instinctive sense of place he felt for his homeland.

Morris's relationship with his home country offers us an insight into the man,

not only as artist and teacher - the two roles for which he is best known; but also as advocate, as promoter, as political representative. He was a man who empathised with the people and recognised their needs and his own responsibilities, and yet often felt desperately powerless to change the situation. However, he did persist in his fight for the right of man to live by more than bread alone.[15] He ensured that even if the people did not have enough to eat during the Depression in the South Wales Valleys, then they could strive for a life which embraced art and culture and enabled them to rise above the harsh realities of the daily grind that was life. In this way Morris did indeed help to save the lives of his people, not only through his pocket, in the rent he paid to the families he stayed with, but through his teaching and support of fellow artists and in his belief that the people of Wales deserved as much right to a cultural life and heritage as everyone else.

Notes

1 Cedric Morris Retrospective Exhibition Catalogue, Welsh Arts Council/National Museum of Wales, 1968, p. 3.

2 TGA 8317.1.4.52. All letters quoted from are held in the Tate Archive, London.

3 He continues, 'Grenfel the MP said to me after his lecture – do you realise that one of the worst spots in S.Wales bears your name & I said yes – I was there yesterday – then he said – I was born there & I worked 23 years underground – then he said Morris of Swansea has gone & Morris of Swansea has come back – so I said Morris of Swansea is dead & he said I dont think so – it was rather like talking to the headmaster at school.' Letter dated August 8 1935. TGA 8317.1.4.94.

4 This included Clough Williams-Ellis, creator of Portmeirion; Wynne Cemlyn-Jones, barrister and writer; Isaac Williams, then Keeper of Art at the National Museum of Wales and the sisters Frances Byng-Stamper and Caroline Byng-Lucas.

5 After the success of the 1935 touring exhibition and the subsequent exhibition at the National Eisteddfod in Fishguard in 1936, a decision was made to set up a Contemporary Art Society for Wales (CASW). The inaugural meeting was held at the Great Western Station Hotel in Paddington on 16 April 1937. Phyllis Bowen, a friend of Morris's and member of CASW also remarked in a letter of October 1983 that the idea for the Society had first been discussed at the Pound and that Augustus John and Cedric Morris had also discussed it at Laugharne Castle and later consulted with Frances Byng-Stamper, who lived nearby at Manorbier Castle. For further information on the CASW see Contemporary Art Society for Wales 50th Anniversary Exhibition Catalogue, 1987, National Museum of Wales, Cardiff.

6 TGA 8317.1.2.11

7 As well as being the 1935 exhibition secretary and the organiser of the 1936 Eisteddfod exhibition, Frances Byng-Stamper was a member of the Contemporary Art Society for Wales for over thirty years and became a Vice-President in 1961. In the same year she initiated and financed a competition open to Welsh artists (the Byng-Stamper Prize) which was judged by Sir Kenneth Clark and won by Will Roberts for the work 'Farm near Cimla'. This work is now in the collection of the National Museums & Galleries of Wales. Byng-Stamper lived for many years in Manorbier Castle, a place where Morris often stayed. Her sister, Caroline Lucas, was an artist herself. In 1935, the year of the touring exhibitions, when Morris and Byng-Stamper were working closely together, he painted a portrait of the two sisters, which he entitled 'The Sisters' and often referred to as 'The English Upper Classes' (no.24, p.64). The painting is a striking one, but not particularly flattering to the sitters, who took great offence. They left Wales in 1939, moved to Lewes and opened Miller's Gallery. For further information on the sisters and their work, see Diana Crook, *The Ladies of Miller's*, 1996, Dale House Press, Lewes.

8 TGA 8317.1.4.91

9 Quoted from a letter written in July 1938, TGA 8317.1.4.92

10 TGA 8317.1.4.93.

11 TGA 8317.1.4.106

12 In a letter of 13 August 1935, he writes, 'Just had supper – great jubilation a rabbit appeared from somewhere and six people had supper off it – me one of them – they only have meat once a week so this was extra – and the once a week ration is a very small very thin mutton chop - I have been wondering what has been happening to my 30/- and today it came out – they have been saving it for the winter to buy coal – in this land of coal they have to go cold in the winter... I shall be glad to get away – every day one sees more and more of it – the reason why I cannot get a room up the Valley is because they all crowd together in the occupied houses to save the rent – there is no room but plenty of empty cottages – all this and much more in the 'fat vale of Glamorgan' plenty everywhere and the people have not enough to eat – either I am going mad or the rest of the world is.' TGA 8317.1.4.95.

13 The beginnings of these Educational Settlements can be traced back to 1901 when staff at the University College of Cardiff became interested in 'extension' work (the provision of an educational presence outside the walls of the University and within the community) and set up a settlement in Splott. These settlements grew in number, especially during the 1920s and 1930s in South Wales, when the Depression made it all the more necessary to provide opportunities for local communities to occupy themselves in different ways, learn new skills and support each other during what were very stressful times. For further information on Educational Settlements see Keith Davies, *Classes, Colleges and Communities: Aspects of a hundred years of adult education in the South Wales Valleys*, 2002 (as yet unpublished).

14 A retrospective of his work was held at the National Museum in Cardiff in 1968. Lett-Haines wrote the introduction to the catalogue.

15 In an interview broadcast from Cardiff on 21 February 1947, he was heard to state these exact words – that 'the people of Wales should be frequently reminded that 'man does not live by bread alone". This echoes the statement issued by Frances Byng-Stamper in 1935 on behalf of the organisers of the Welsh Contemporary Art Exhibition.

Fig. 12. Lett Haines in his studio at Benton End, 1974

Lett Haines: The Artist in the Airship

Nicholas Thornton

In 1926 Lett Haines was selected as the only British artist in the *International Exhibition* of modern art held at the Brooklyn Museum, New York. The exhibition, which featured internationally acclaimed artists including Fernand Léger, Joan Mirò, Pablo Picasso, Juan Gris and Georgia O'Keefe, was intended as a survey of Modernist art in the United States and Europe. In the catalogue, Katherine Dreier described Lett Haines as:

> the only Englishman whose work I have seen or come across which shows an understanding of what the Modernists claim as their point of view. He must live in an airship, as he is back and forth between London and Paris so much.[1]

Lett's inclusion in the exhibition, alongside this statement, clearly shows that the curators at the Brooklyn Museum viewed his work as worthy of consideration alongside the work of artists whose place has now been firmly established in the history of twentieth century art. Given this, one is led to question why Lett has so consistently been overlooked in histories of British art. On the occasions when his

work has been discussed it has tended to be mentioned in passing as an adjunct to discussions of the life and work of his partner Cedric Morris. This essay seeks to address this issue and provide an introduction to an artist whose work merits focused attention.

The biographical details of Lett's early life remain uncertain and only become clearer following his meeting with Cedric. They met in November 1918 and fell immediately in love. In 1919 Lett separated from his second wife Aimée to start a turbulent, yet nonetheless devoted relationship with Cedric, which lasted until Lett's death in 1978. In common with Cedric, Lett had minimal formal training in the visual arts. Describing himself as a 'late developer' as an artist, he had reached the age of 24 before he was able to dedicate his life 'freely to the practice of the fine arts.'[2] Lett and Cedric were becoming increasingly serious artists by the time they moved to Newlyn, Cornwall in 1919 and then to Paris in early 1921. Although they frequently returned to London and travelled widely in Europe and North Africa, it was Paris that Lett described as his 'headquarters for the next ten years'.[3] During this period Lett enjoyed one of the most sustained exposures to European modernism of any British artist in the 1920s; it is this exposure that provides a key to understanding his subsequent work.

In an autobiographical statement dating from 1969 Lett declared that his main influences: 'apart from the Classical were Wyndham Lewis in London 1918, Georgio de Chirico in Italy 1922, W.Kandinsky in Germany 1923 and Pablo Picasso in France.'[4] The extent to which Lett had access to these artists and their work remains uncertain, although we know that he met Wyndham Lewis in London and that Lewis was a visitor to their Cornish home during 1919. If he did not actually meet the other three artists, it is very likely that he would have had opportunities to see their work during his travels in Italy, Germany and France. Diaries and notebooks from the 1920s reveal an extensive range of contacts in both the Parisian artistic and literary communities that included Man Ray, Constantin Brancusi, Ossip Zadkine, Jean Cocteau and Ernest Hemingway.[5] Key to understanding the development of Lett's work is his sophisticated knowledge of a wide range of avant-garde styles. Unlike Cedric, who worked almost exclusively within an English tradition, Lett can be seen to have responded to Wyndham Lewis's call for British artists in the 1920s to regard themselves as 'European first, and to paint and think for that wider audience.'[6]

Fig. 13. Lett Haines, early 1930s

Composition 1922 (no.57, p.80), one of Lett's most important works from the 1920s, clearly reveals his willingness to investigate the latest developments in European art. The painting can be viewed as a knowing amalgamation of the latest avant-garde tendencies, negotiating pastiche with an individual and convincing composition. A ship or train's funnel, a recurring image in art of the machine age, dominates the foreground; it is represented against an imaginary landscape constructed predominantly from simplified geometric forms. The interlocking light and dark forms in the top-left, together with stylised shading on the cylindrical forms, suggest a knowledge of Purist paintings of the early 1920s by Charles-Édouard Jeanneret and Amédée Ozenfant, as well as Léger's paintings of the same period.[7]

However, the differences between *Composition* and the work of these artists are as marked as the similarities. Whilst the Purists preferred subdued tones and flattened their simplified forms against the picture plane, Lett opted for a brighter palette, positioning his forms in different layers of pictorial space. *Composition* is also far removed from the Purists' aim to produce paintings informed by rational process and the search for logical order. The abstract concentric circles that appear to be floating in the right foreground, which are themselves redolent of the Orphic Cubism of Sonia and Robert Delaunay, contribute in the creation of a sense of other-worldly strangeness that is also present in other motifs in the painting.[8] For instance the red flag above the small building on the horizon line relates to de Chirico's employment of similar flags in a number of his 'metaphysical' paintings including *Mystery and Melancholy of a Street* 1913 . We see that Lett had little interest in following a single movement or method and was prepared to integrate different styles and approaches within a single work. *Composition* creates an individual statement by suggesting two opposing directions in Paris art of the 1920s: the rationality of Purism and the enigmatic mystery of de Chirico.

Lett's ability to adopt and manipulate a range of modernist sources contrasts with Cedric's approach. Although Cedric briefly experimented with avant-garde forms in the mid-1920s, most successfully in abstracts such as *Experiment in Textures* 1923 (no.6, p.50), his work was largely uninfluenced by progressive art.[9] On occasions when modern forms are referenced, as in *Golden Auntie* 1923 (no.7, p.51), they appear to be used almost for the purpose of parody. The futuristic architectural forms in *Golden Auntie*, which closely resemble the architecture in Lett's paintings such as *Amusement* 1922 (no.59), are painted with an unsophisticated directness. The resulting awkwardness serves to undermine the very avant-garde sophistication that it mimics. Such a reading of *Golden Auntie* is reinforced by the fact that the figure in the suit is Lett waiting for his legacy following the death of a relative. Cedric has represented his lover within a 'modernist landscape' reminiscent of Lett's own work.

The contrast in their approach and styles gives us an insight into their contrasting reception in Britain in the 1920s. The radicalism that had been a feature of British art prior to the outbreak of the First World War had largely disappeared by the 1920s. 'Progressive' art in Britain was represented by the safe modernism of Bloomsbury post-impressionism that, although looking towards Paris for inspiration, largely seemed to ignore developments since Cubism. Given this climate it would be difficult to imagine Lett's sophisticated modernism securing much critical acclaim. Cedric's work, however, was ideally placed for a more favourable reception.[10] The direct, almost naive simplicity of paintings such as *Llanmadoc Hill, Gower Peninsula* 1928 (no.16, p.32) aligned his work closely with the *faux-naïf* styles of Christopher Wood, Ben Nicholson and their colleagues in the 7&5 Society. This would have stood Cedric in good stead for the development of his career in the 1920s and 30s.[11]

Analysis of Lett's Parisian years has revealed an artist who, although detached from theories and manifestos, understood and was willing to learn from the latest developments. One of the enduring qualities of his work is its surrealist spirit. Paintings such as *Powers in Atrophe* 1922 (no.55, p.79) reveal an affinity with the ideas and imagery of surrealism, even though it was painted two years before surrealism was officially established as a movement. Following his return to Britain in 1926, and eventual move to the relative isolation of East Anglia, Lett continued to remain alive to recent developments in modern art. What is particularly significant about Lett's work in the 1930s is that it retained its affinity with surrealism, and relates to imagery used by British surrealists such as John Banting and Grace Pailthorpe. In his more figurative work of the 1930s Lett's choice and treatment of subject encourages comparison with Edward Burra's work from the same period. They both worked almost exclusively on paper and produced art that was led by imaginative expression and a creative theatricality. Whilst Burra had closer connections with the English surrealists than Lett, he was still a marginal figure in the group's activity.

Although Lett did have informal contact with official members of the British surrealist group, most notably through his long standing friendship with John Banting, he appears to have never exhibited with the group or had any official dealings with the movement.[12] His surrealism is suggested by his adoption of generalised themes that would have appealed to the surrealist sensibility: eroticism, spiritualism, and an exotic 'primitivism'. *The Dark Horse* 1934 (no.64, p.76) appears initially to be a largely representational scene of a North African town. Closer inspection reveals the work to be loaded with inexplicable motifs and events. The architecture above the main arches reveals a 'hidden city', whilst the calligraphy and pictograms on the left of the scene are inscriptions in a strange, vaguely Arabic, language. In the bottom-right bodies are revealed writhing in agony or ecstasy in a hidden cellar. The whole scene is punctuated with doorways and openings that suggest the possibility of moving into areas beyond the rational world.

The Martyrdom of Purple Hampton 1955 (no.66), conveys a violent eroticism that can also be aligned to aspects of surrealist theory and art. Elements in this work introduce Lett's loose, calligraphic style which he also adopted as a technique in his most abstract work. Seemingly led by chance effects and the possibility of meaning created through association, works such as *Untitled (Automatic Drawing)* c.1965 (no.68) are Lett's most abstract expressions of a surrealist spirit.

Although Lett moves through an eclectic range of styles and approaches, the human figure is his most enduring subject. In *Composition* 1922 (no.57) the subject is treated in an abstract manner; the fluid grey forms in the centre-right suggest the head and shoulders of a figure, whilst a human form is also suggested, this time in a more geometric way, in the bottom left. In *Powers in Atrophe*, reference to the human form is more explicit; the tiny figure of a man is dwarfed by a staircase leading into a strange 'architecture' composed of organic forms punctuated

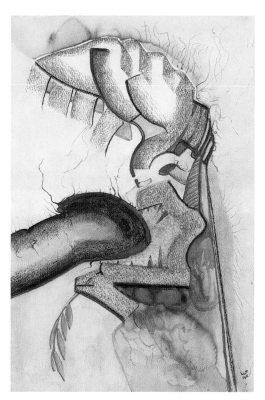

Lett Haines *The Martyrdom of Purple Hampton* 1955 (no. 66)

with prominent eyes. In the bottom right of this work the outline of a seated male nude is also clearly discernable. These two ways of representing the human figure - dwarfed by an imaginative architectural structure and reduced to an enigmatic outline - are recurring motifs in Lett's work of the 1920s . The reduction of the human form to an outline remained a common way of representing the body in Lett's later work as well. For example in *Untitled (Flowers, Window and Figures)* 1957 (no.67) the flowers are integrated with a group of tumbling figures to create an orgiastic celebration of human and floral fecundity.

During the 1930s Lett's output seems to have slowed and he exhibited less regularly. This can in part be explained by the circumstances of his life and in particular the subjugation of his own work in order to further Cedric's career. From 1937 he was fully involved in managing the East Anglia School of Painting and Drawing. As Lett himself remarked in 1969: 'In 1937 I founded the East Anglia School of Painting and Drawing at Dedham in Essex...which has absorbed the greatest part of my energies since.'[13] Lett managed the School, carried out all the associated administration, and undertook many of the domestic duties involved in running the house. The most notable example are the meals that he produced on a daily basis at Benton End; an excellent cook, he would normally take responsibility for cooking two meals a day. Such selfless work on behalf of the School, the students and

Cedric inevitably compromised the amount of time that he was able to devote to his own work. It is perhaps no coincidence that he was able to produce more work during the 1960s when Benton End was no longer running as a School and Millie Hayes had taken over a number of the domestic duties.

This late flowering in Lett's career saw a significant switch in his working practices. Although he continued to work on paper, his main focus from the mid-1960s onwards became a series of extraordinarily inventive sculptures that the artist grouped under the generic title *petites sculptures*. Although earlier in his career Lett had produced a number of small sculptures including *Dieties of the Lake (Tunisia)* 1925 (no.71) and *Mud Pie* c.1930 (no.72), this was his first sustained period of working in three dimensions.[14] Joan Warburton, a regular visitor to Benton End, makes an anecdotal, yet nonetheless revealing reference to Lett's work during this period in her diary: 'There he is upstairs supping gin, smoking cigars, making obscene "toys" out of *objects-trouvé*, and painting slowly.'[15]

What is particularly significant about Lett's 'obscene toys' is his imaginative use of found objects. There is a certain playful, irreverent nature to these works, that is distinctly surreal. Usually these materials were 'found' in the immediate vicinity of Benton End - bones from the cooking pot or vegetables from the garden. In *Baked Carrot* (no.76) the vegetable, complete with veins made from string, has been mounted onto a base so that it points upwards in a defiantly phallic gesture. In *Ensemble du Banquet* (no.80) bones have been painted to create a serpent like creature, whilst in *Petit Sculpture (Jerusalem Artichoke)* (no.77) doll's eyes have been added to the root to create another imaginatively macabre monster. Lett's light-hearted use of materials and reference to subjects and themes explored in earlier work make the *petites-sculptures* a humorous but significant *résumé* of many of his key ideas and interests. A resonance from this work may be seen in the later sculptural work of one of Lett's most celebrated students, Maggi Hambling.

What is particularly remarkable about the work Lett produced during his sixty-year career is its spirit of experimentation and enquiry. He was an artist who was able to observe and understand a range of artistic sources to produce work that retained a distinctive originality. He was never prepared to further his career by working within a fashionable or current style, yet sacrificed so many of his own ambitions to promote the EASPD, its students and above all the work of Cedric. The strength and diversity of Lett's work, revealed by this exhibition and the accompanying publication, will hopefully encourage us all to take a closer look at his work and accord him his rightful place in the history of twentieth century British art.[16]

Lett Haines *Selection of Petites Scuptures* (Nos 75-80)

Notes

1 Katherine S. Dreier, *International Exhibition*, exh. cat., Brooklyn Museum, New York, 1926
Lett's papers are now held in the Hyman Kreitman Research Centre at Tate Britain, as part of the Morris Archive (TGA 8317)

2 Lett Haines, Unpublished Account of Artistic Career, 1969   TGA 8317.6.3.2

3 TGA 8317.6.3.2

4 TGA 8317.6.3.2

5 A notebook, containing lists of events and people under annual headings, includes Kiki Smith, Man Ray, Peggy Guggenheim, Nancy Cunard, Juan Gris and Ossip Zadkine as the 'dramatis personae' of Lett's years in Paris. (See TGA 8317.7.3.5). See Richard Morphet, *Cedric Morris*, exh. cat., Tate Gallery, 1984 pp.22-26 for further discussion of Cedric and Lett's life and contacts in Paris during the 1920s.

6 Wyndham Lewis, Letter to John Quinn, 14 June 1920. Quoted in Charles Harrison, *English Art and Modernism 1900-1939*, Yale University Press, 1981, p.148

7 Lett would have had plenty of opportunities to see examples of Léger's work. Morris studied under Léger at the Académies Moderne and he also was part of their social circle in Paris. See Morphet (1984), p.23

8 In particular Sonia and Robert Delaunay's studies of Parisian streetlights 1913-14.

9 Although in subject, style and media there are few similarities between Cedric and Lett's work, the work produced in the early to mid-1920s does reveal a degree of interchange. Lett's technique of picking out abstract and figurative forms by tracing linear motifs over the main composition (for example see nos 55 and 59) is also used adopted by Cedric. For example in Cedric's *The Celtic Twilight* 1924 (illustrated Morphet (1984), p.30) he uses the technique to reveal ghostly forms of people and a cow.

10 It should also be noted that a motivating factor in Lett's decision to leave Paris in 1926, was his wish to further Cedric's career which he felt could be best served by returning to live and work in Britain.

11 For discussion of the shifts in attitudes to progressive art and traditional values during this period see Richard Morphet, 'Realism in English Art, 1919-1939' in *Cahiers du Musée National d'Art Moderne*, nos.7/8, 1981 pp.322-345

12 Lett knew Banting from the early 1920s. Cedric painted a portrait of him in 1923 (illustrated Morphet (1984), p.24) and they shared the same social circle in Paris. He was also a regular visitor to The Pound during the 1930s. Maggi Hambling recalls that Lett referred to himself as an 'English Surrealist' (Maggi Hambling, unpublished interview with Ben Tufnell, 30 May 1997)

13 TGA 8317.6.3.2

14 The catalogue of Lett's solo exhibition at the Minories, Colchester in 1974 lists 55 examples of *petites sculptures* produced between 1965-74.

15 Joan Warburton, Diary 19 March 1973, TGA 968.2

16 I would like to thank Maggi Hambling, Glyn Morgan, Gwynneth Reynolds, Robert Short and Bod Wright for their memories of the EASPD and their insight into the life and work of Lett Haines.

The Artists

Sir Cedric Morris 1889-1982

Biography

Cedric Lockwood Morris was born in 1889 near Swansea, South Wales. His father, George Morris, and mother Wilhelmina, both came from wealthy families with strong industrial and mining interests in South Wales. In 1947 Cedric succeeded to the family baronetcy, becoming the 9th Baronet. He remained proud of his Welsh roots and was a life-long supporter of the arts in Wales. He was a founder of the Contemporary Art Society for Wales and President of the South Wales Art Society. He was also a co-founder of the Colchester Art Society in 1946.

After attending Charterhouse he worked and travelled in North America. In 1914 he went to Paris and enrolled at the Académie Delacluse in Montparnesse to study art. The outbreak of the First World War interrupted these studies, and failing an army medical, he spent much of the War training horses for the military.

In London in November 1918 he met Arthur Lett-Haines who became his life-long partner. They lived in Newlyn, Cornwall from 1919-20 and were based in Paris from 1920-26, travelling widely in Europe and North Africa, before moving back to London, where Morris had a series of extremely successful exhibitions.

In 1929 they rented The Pound, near Higham, Suffolk and in 1930 they left London and used the farmhouse as their permanent base, establishing the EASPD there in 1937. In 1940, following the fire at the Dedham School, they moved to Benton End, Hadleigh which became both their home and the premises of the EASPD.

After a period of experimentation 1919-26 Morris' work was, to a remarkable degree, stylistically consistent for the rest of his career. His painting is characterised by direct observation, lively surface texture and intense colour. His principal subjects were flowers, birds, portraits, still lives and landscapes.

Selected Exhibitions

1922 Bragaglia Casa d'Arte, Rome (with Lett Haines)

1928 Koninklijke Kunstzaal, The Hague

1928, 1930, 1934 Arthur Tooth & Sons, London

1938 *Portraits*, Guggenheim Jeune, London

1968 National Museum of Wales, Cardiff

1980 The Minories, Colchester

1984 Tate Gallery, London; National Museum of Wales, Cardiff; The Minories, Colchester

1990 Redfern Gallery, London

Selected Bibliography

RH Wilenski, 'Introduction' in *Stoneware Pottery* by *WS Murray*, *Paintings & Drawings by Cedric Morris*, exh. cat., Arts League of Service, London 1924

Cedric Morris, '*Concerning Flower Painting*' in *The Studio* CXXIII May 1942 pp. 121-132

Ronald Blythe, 'Introduction' in *Sir Cedric Morris*, exh. cat. The Minories 1980

Richard Morphet, *Cedric Morris*, exh. cat., Tate Gallery 1984

5. Cedric Morris, *Patisseries and a Croissant*, c.1922

6. Cedric Morris, *Experiment in Textures*, 1923

9. Cedric Morris, *The Dancing Sailor*, 1925

7. Cedric Morris, *Golden Auntie*, 1923

13. Cedric Morris, *From a Bedroom Window at 45 Brook Street, W.1.*, 1926

20. Cedric Morris, *The River Stour in Flood,* 1930

23. Cedric Morris, *Solva*, 1934

26. Cedric Morris, *Caeharris Post Office, Dowlais,* 1935

36. Cedric Morris, *Wartime Garden* c. 1944

35. Cedric Morris, *The Eggs*, 1944

40. Cedric Morris, *Ratatouille*, 1954

15. Cedric Morris, *Birds of the Air*, 1928

41. Cedric Morris, *Landscape of Shame*, c.1960

1. Cedric Morris, *Self Portrait*, 1919

2. Cedric Morris, *Arthur Lett Haines*, 1919

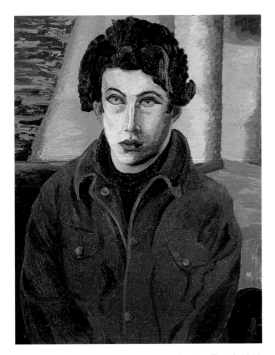

31. Cedric Morris, *Lucian Freud*, 1940

18. Cedric Morris, *Self Portrait*, 1930

8. Cedric Morris, *Mary Butts*, 1924

10. Cedric Morris, *The Swiss Visitor*, 1925

24. Cedric Morris, *The Sisters (The English Upper Classes)*, 1935

30. Cedric Morris, *David and Barbara Carr*, c.1940

28. Cedric Morris, *Antonia White*, 1936

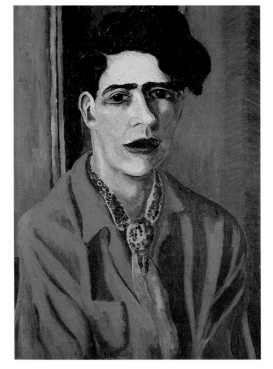

38. Cedric Morris, *Glyn Morgan*, 1949

49.Cedric Morris, *Still Life*, 1921

51. Cedric Morris, *Fascists in Rome*, 1922

50. Cedric Morris, *A Roman Café*, 1922

47. Cedric Morris, *Café Scene*, 1921

39. Cedric Morris, *Blackbird and Flowers*, 1952

19. Cedric Morris, *Black Tulip*, c.1930

44. Cedric Morris, *Flowers in a Blue Pot*, 1966

33. Cedric Morris, *Irises*, 1941

34. Cedric Morris, *Iris Seedlings*, 1943

Arthur Lett Haines 1894-1978

Biography

Arthur Lett was born in London in 1894. In 1916, following the death of his father, he changed his name by deed poll, adding the surname of his stepfather Sydney Haines to his own surname. In later life he dropped his Christian name; using Lett as his first name he subsequently became known to all as Lett Haines.

Lett was married to his second wife Aimée (his first wife having died when Lett was just seventeen years old) when he met Cedric Morris in November 1918. They fell immediately in love and Lett separated from Aimée in 1919 to start a turbulent, yet nonetheless devoted relationship with Morris, which lasted for the remainder of their lives. In common with Morris, Lett had numerous affairs, including a long-term relationship with artist and writer Kathleen Hale.

He established the EASPD in 1937 and ran the School, dealing with all the managerial and administrative duties. He was an accomplished cook and the meals he produced are remembered both for the exotic excellence of the food and as important social occasions in Benton End life. He also took a lead in promoting and managing Morris' career, enabling him to focus on his own painting and gardening.

Lett's work is notable for his commitment to experimentation. As such he is difficult to categorise, although he called himself an 'English surrealist'. He primarily worked in watercolour on paper, but also made paintings in oil, collages, textile designs, and sculptures.

Lett's papers in the Tate Archive reveal he was a writer as well as an artist. Poems and plays accompany a range of non-fiction dealing with a broad range of subjects. He was an intellectual – sophisticated, cosmopolitan and a perceptive judge of character. He was renowned for his intelligence, good advice and humour and was (ironically) called 'Father' by many of the students.

Selected Exhibitions

1922 Bragaglia Casa d'Arte, Rome (with Cedric Morris)

1926 *Cedric Morris, Lett Haines: English Moderns*, Little Review Gallery, New York

1926 Gallerie Leven, Palais Royale, Paris

1926 *International Exhibition*, Museum of Modern Art, Brooklyn, New York

1931 St George's Gallery, London

1936 Picture Hire Limited, London

1966, 1974 Minories, Colchester

1984 *Paintings Drawings and Petites Sculptures*, Redfern Gallery, London

Selected Bibliography

Katherine S. Dreier, *International Exhibition*, Museum of Modern Art, Brooklyn, New York 1926

Lett Haines: Petites Sculptures 1965-74, Paintings and Drawings 1919-74, exh. cat. The Minories 1974

Richard Morphet, 'Introduction' in *Arthur Lett-Haines: Paintings Drawings and Petites Sculptures,* exh. cat., Redfern Gallery, London 1984

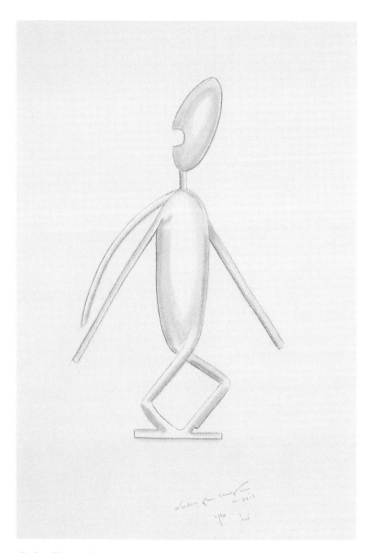

54. Lett Haines, *Etude pour Sculpture en Bois*, 1920

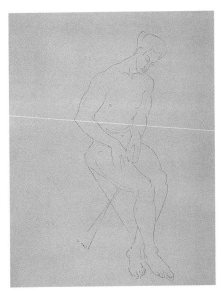

60. Lett Haines, *Study of Cedric Morris*, 1925

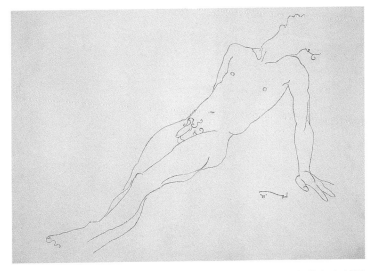

61. Lett Haines, *Study of Cedric Morris (Reclining)*, 1925

53. Lett Haines, *Old Brighton Railway Station*, 1920

64. Lett Haines, *The Dark Horse*, 1934

62. Lett Haines, *The Lion Hunt*, 1929

63. Lett Haines, *The Escape*, 1931

58. Lett Haines, *Composition*, 1923

78

55. Lett Haines, *Powers in Atrophe*, 1922

57. Lett Haines, *Composition*, 1922

73. Lett Haines, *Regardant*, 1959

74. Lett Haines, *Witch Fetish (Portrait of Maggi)* 1962

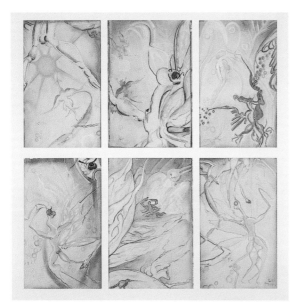

70. Lett Haines, *Vue d'une Fenêtre*, 1967

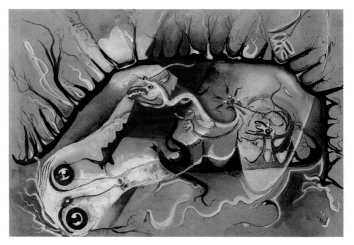

69. Lett Haines, *Poor Dolly*, 1966

Frances Hodgkins 1869-1947

Biography

Born in 1869 in Dunedin, New Zealand, Hodgkins attended Dunedin School of Art 1895-6. In 1901-03 she travelled in Europe and Morocco. She returned to Europe in 1906, teaching painting in a number of European countries before settling in Paris in 1908. In 1913, after returning briefly to New Zealand, she settled in St.Ives, Cornwall, which became her base until 1920.

In the 1920s she moved between France and England, but in 1928 made a more permanent home in London in a bid to secure wider recognition for her work. During the 1930s she painted in various locations in Britain including Suffolk, Cornwall and Wales. In 1939 she settled in Corfe Castle, Dorset, which was to be her base for the remainder of her life.

Hodgkins' acquaintance with Lett Haines and Morris became friendship in 1919-20 when they were all living in Cornwall. Both men encouraged Hodgkins in her artistic ambitions and during the 1920s introduced her to a number of galleries and dealers, and proposed her for membership of the 7&5. On 24 February 1930 she wrote to Lucy Wertheim: 'the fact that I am working here today in a state of comparative liberty & independence I very largely owe to the friendship of Lett & Cedric.' She painted Lett's portrait in Tréboul in 1927 (sold at Christies 12 March 1993, lot 13) and a portrait of Morris (no.81) in 1930, whilst staying at The Pound.

In 1940 she represented Britain at the Venice Biennale and her reputation as a leading British artist was established.

Selected Exhibitions

1933, 1937, 1940, 1943, 1946 Lefevre Gallery, London

1935, 1941, 1956, Leicester Galleries, London

1952 *Ethel Walker, Frances Hodgkins, Gwen John*, Tate Gallery, London

1954, 1959, 1969, 1979, 1991, 1994 Auckland City Art Gallery, New Zealand

Selected Publications

Myfanwy Evans, *Frances Hodgkins*, Penguin Modern Painters 1948

EH McCormick, *Portrait of Frances Hodgkins*, Oxford University Press 1981

Linda Gill ed., *The Letters of Frances Hodgkins*, Auckland University Press 1993

Iain Buchanan, Michael Dunn and Elizabeth Eastmond ed., *Frances Hodgkins: Paintings and Drawings*, Thames and Hudson 1995

81. Frances Hodgkins, *Man with Macaw (Portrait of Cedric Morris)*, 1930

82. Frances Hodgkins, *Flatford Mill*, 1930

Lucy Harwood 1893-1972

Biography

Born in 1893 at Belstead Park, near Ipswich, Lucy Harwood lived all her life in Suffolk. She studied at the Slade School of Art before 1914 and according to Lett Haines 'later claimed, inaccurately, that she had been expelled as deficient in drawing....'. She studied at the EASPD from 1937; she was to remain devoted to Morris and Lett Haines and always showed her finished work to them for their approval.

Harwood painted her surroundings: the local landscape, still lives of flowers and vegetables, portraits of fellow students and local people. Her best work is characterised by directness, strong colour and a certain *naiveté* or lack of sophistication that communicates a passionate and very personal response to the subject. Harwood suffered from hallucinations and paralysis in her right side. This forced her to paint with her left hand and may account for the rugged, rather unorthodox quality of her work.

Morris was clearly a strong influence but according to Lett she also 'felt an affinity to Vincent Van Gogh, Amedeo Modigliani, Paul Gauguin, Chaïm Soutine and others' – artists whose work is notable for its directness and expressiveness. Indeed, Harwood was known as the 'Van Gogh of Suffolk' and a work such as *Landscape with Gulls* (no.84) is clearly related to Van Gogh's *Wheatfield with Crows* 1890, in both subject and handling.

Selected Exhibitions

1952 Flint House Galleries, Norwich

1975 The Minories, Colchester

1985, 1987, 1989 Sally Hunter Fine Art, London

Publications

Arthur Lett Haines 'Introduction' in *Lucy Harwood, Commemorative Exhibition*, exh. cat., The Minories 1975

83. Lucy Harwood, *Still Life with Fish*, c.1940

84. Lucy Harwood, *Landscape with Gulls*, n.d.

85. Lucy Harwood, *The Signal* n.d.

David Carr 1915-68

Biography

David Carr was born in Wimbledon, London, in 1915. In 1934, after attending Uppingham School he entered the family business - Peak Frean biscuits. In 1936, disillusioned with the commercial world, he attended Exeter College, Oxford, to study history. During this period he visited Italy where exposure to Italian Art and architecture led to his decision to leave Oxford and pursue a career as an artist.

In 1939 he attended the Byam Shaw Art School, London. Later in the same year he enrolled at the EASPD and was a live-in student for three years. He was introduced to the School by fellow pupil Barbara Gilligan, whom he married in 1942. Following a period living in Somerset, they bought Starston Hall, a large farmhouse near Harleston in Norfolk where Carr established his studio in the attic room. He continued to make frequent visits to Benton End. In 1956 he co-founded the Norfolk Contemporary Art Society.

Carr's early work, such as the portraits of Lowestoft fishermen painted in the late 1940s, reveals Morris' influence, particularly in their directness, simplicity of forms and concern with surface texture. Carr was an early supporter of Lowry, whose work was also an influence particularly in the handling of paint, use of colour, and the exploration of imagery of social deprivation. The tense strangeness in his portraits of the 1940s is also reminiscent of Freud's work of the period.

Carr's choice of subject was in part motivated by social concerns. In 1949, following studies of workers in the family biscuit factory, he embarked on his *Man and Machine* series representing workers conflated with mechanical forms (no.90). His interest in this subject is mirrored in the work of his great friend Prunella Clough who explored similar themes in the 1950s. In the 1960s Carr started to paint in watercolour, often in 'themed' sketchbooks. These inventive studies indicate a movement towards abstraction. In 1967 Carr visited New York and produced sculptures and abstract studies based on his experience of the City.

Selected Exhibitions

1954 *British Painting & Sculpture*, Whitechapel Art Gallery

1969 Berthe Schaefer Gallery, New York

1972 *Drawings, Watercolours, Paintings and Sculpture*, Castle Museum, Norwich

1987 Mayor Gallery, London

1997 *David Carr & Prunella Clough: Works 1945-64*, Austin Desmond Fine Art, London

Publications

Barbara Carr and Eric Fowler, *Drawings, Watercolours, Paintings and Sculpture by David Carr*, exh cat, Castle Museum, Norwich 1972

Bryan Robertson and Ronald Alley, *David Carr: The Discovery of an Artist*, Quartet Books 1987

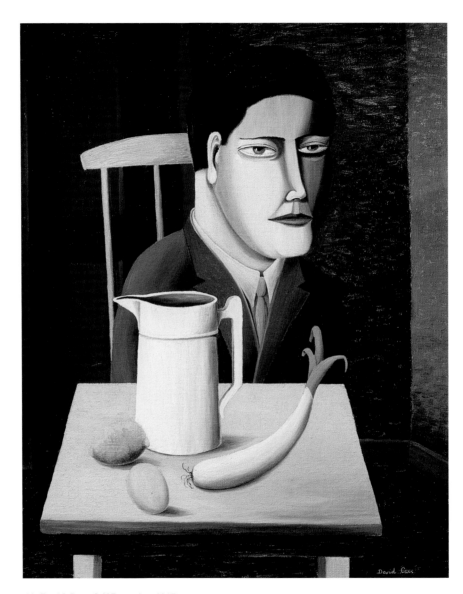

89. David Carr, *Self-Portrait*, c.1947

90. David Carr, *Man and Machine VI*, c.1952

Lucian Freud b.1922

Biography

Born in 1922 in Berlin, the grandson of
Sigmund Freud. The family moved to
Britain in 1933 and Freud became a
naturalised British subject in 1939. He
attended Dartington Hall School and the
Central School of Arts and Crafts before
joining the EASPD in 1939, where he was
particularly close to fellow students David
Carr and David Kentish (with whom he
collaborated on a number of works).

Freud's time at the EASPD was formative -
Morris was without doubt the most
important influence on his early work –
and many of his concerns from this period
recur in his later work. For example, the
subject of his paintings – portraits, still
lives, birds and animals – and the frontal
treatment of them as well as a concern
with surface texture, all recall Morris.
Freud's portraiture is particularly indebted
to Morris' example in its use of
dispassionate observation to create an
unnerving sense of psychological
examination, and even malaise.

In 1941 Freud briefly joined the merchant
navy; by 1942 he was based in London,
where he shared a flat with the painter
John Craxton. At this point his work
became more overtly engaged with
Surrealism (see for example *Tenby
Harbour* 1944 (no.94), which
anthropomorphises a rock formation in the
harbour), although this had already been
an interest in the late 1930s.

Freud's later career is well documented. In
1981 he contributed a foreword to the
catalogue of Morris' exhibition at Blond
Fine Art, writing 'Cedric taught me to paint
and more important to keep at it. He did
not say much, but let me watch him at
work. I have always admired his paintings
and everything about him.' More recently
he told William Feaver 'I thought Cedric
was a real painter. Dense and
extraordinary. Terrific limitations.'

Selected Exhibitions

1944 Lefevre Gallery, London

1974 Retrospective organised by Arts Council: Hayward Gallery, London and tour

1987-88 *Lucian Freud Paintings*, retrospective organised by British Council: Hirschorn Museum & Sculpture Garden, Washington DC; Musée National d'Art Moderne, Paris; Hayward Gallery, London; Neue Nationalgalerie, Berlin

1997 *Early Works*, Scottish National Gallery of Modern Art, Edinburgh

2002-03 Tate Britain, London; La Caixa, Barcelona; LACMA, Los Angeles

Selected Publications

Lucian Freud 'Some Thoughts on Painting', *Encounter* July 1954 Vol.3 No.1 p.23

Lawrence Gowing, *Lucian Freud*, Thames & Hudson 1982

Bruce Bernard and Derek Birdsall, *Lucian Freud*, Jonathan Cape 1996

Richard Calvocoressi, *Lucian Freud: Early Works*, exh cat, SNGMA Edinburgh 1997

William Feaver, *Lucian Freud*, exh. cat., Tate 2002

91. Lucian Freud, *Woman with Rejected Suitors*, 1939

92. Lucian Freud, *Cedric Morris*, 1940

93. Lucian Freud, *Memory of London*, 1940

94. Lucian Freud, *Tenby Harbour*, 1944

Glyn Morgan b.1926

Biography

Born in 1926 in Pontypridd, Wales, Morgan studied at Cardiff School of Art with Ceri Richards from 1942-44 and Camberwell School of Art from 1947-48. Morgan was introduced to Morris in 1943 by Esther Grainger, who at that time was teaching at the Pontypridd Settlement. He first visited Benton End in the summer of 1944. Morris told him 'You have a disgraceful sense of colour, therefore you might become an artist.' From this point on Morgan made regular visits to Benton End until Morris' death, eventually moving to Hadleigh in 1995.

Morgan's early work was much influenced by Morris, but, following a year spent living in Paris in 1951, when he became interested in the articulation of space and light in the work of Bonnard and Braque (as seen in the *Still Life with Chinese Pot* 1961 (no.97) his work began to move away from that of his teacher. In 1968 he was awarded a Goldsmiths Company Fellowship to work and study in Crete. His painting thereafter became more abstracted and imaginative, using colour and symbolic forms to articulate a sense of place, and to represent subjects drawn from classical myth, as in *The Table of Minos VI* 1971 (no.98).

Morgan's later work has focused on the English and Welsh landscape, in particular that of Suffolk and the Llantony Valley, Wales, which he has been painting for more than twenty years. As in the Cretan works he is concerned to combine topography with intimations of a world that lies beyond visible reality. The examples of Paul Nash, Graham Sutherland and Ceri Richards are apparent in his treatment of overtly 'native' or Celtic themes: the Green Man, standing stones, and auspicious moments in the calendar such as solstice and eclipse.

Selected Exhibitions

1969 Drian Gallery, London

1971 The Minories, Colchester

1985 Archway Gallery, Houston, Texas

1996 *The Green Man*, Chappel Galleries, Essex

1997 *Retrospective*, Y Tabernacl, The Museum of Modern Art, Wales

1998 Brecknock Museum & Gallery, Brecon

1998, 2001 Chappel Galleries, Essex

Publications

Ronald Blythe, *A Vision of Landscape: The Art of Glyn Morgan*, Chappel Monograph 2001

95. Glyn Morgan, *Cedric Morris in his Garden*, c.1957

97. Glyn Morgan, *Still Life with Chinese Pot*, 1961

98. Glyn Morgan, *Table of Minos VI*, 1971

Maggi Hambling b.1945

Biography

Maggi Hambling was born in Sudbury in 1945 and grew up in Hadleigh, Suffolk. Her first meeting with Morris and Lett Haines was in 1960, and she began to paint at Benton End and during the summer holidays. She studied at Ipswich School of Art with Laurence Self and Bernard Reynolds from 1962-64, and from 1964-67 at Camberwell School of Art, with the painter Robert Medley. In 1967-69 she attended the Slade School of Art, where she experimented with conceptual and performance art. She was awarded the Boise Travel Award in 1969 and spent time in New York. She returned to painting in 1972, with an acclaimed series of portraits from memory, of solitary drinkers in pubs.

Hambling has always regarded Lett as her mentor. At Benton End she helped him in the kitchen where she has said she learnt her most important lesson: 'He taught me that your work had to be the priority of your life. He also said (you had to) get into the relationship where your work is your best friend, that you can go to it however depressed you are, however elated you are. Whatever condition you are in, you can go to your work and have a conversation with it.' (*Towards Laughter* p.16).

While Hambling is probably best known for her portraiture (Max Wall, George Melly, Dorothy Hodgkins, Stephen Fry and A.J.P. Taylor are in the National Portrait Gallery), she has, like Lett, remained restlessly inventive. In 1992 she began to make sculpture, first in fired clay and then in bronze. In 1998 her memorial to Oscar Wilde was unveiled in Central London. She has recently painted, drawn and sculpted two series of portraits of her father and Henrietta Moraes.

Selected Exhibitions

1967 *Paintings and Drawings*, Hadleigh Gallery, Suffolk

1981 *Drawings and Paintings on View*, National Gallery, London

1983 *Pictures of Max Wall*, National Portrait Gallery, London

1987 *Maggi Hambling*, Serpentine Gallery, London

1991 *An Eye through a Decade 1981-1991*, Yale Centre for British Art, New Haven

1996 *Sculpture in Bronze*, Marlborough Fine Art, London

2001 *Father*, Morley Gallery, London

2001 *Henrietta Moraes*, Marlborough Fine Art, London

Selected Publications

Mel Gooding, *An Eye Through a Decade*, exh. cat., Yale Centre for British Art 1991

George Melly and Judith Collins, *Towards Laughter*, exh. cat., Northern Centre for Contemporary Art/Lund Humphries 1993

Andrew Lambirth, 'Moments of laughter and death' in *Father*, exh. cat., Morley Gallery, London 2001

John Berger, 'The 235 days', in *Maggi and Henrietta: Drawings of Henrietta Moraes by Maggi Hambling*, Bloomsbury 2001

99. Maggi Hambling, *Rhinoceros, Ipswich Museum*, 1963

100. Maggi Hambling, *Seated Female Nude*, 1963

101. Maggi Hambling, *Ipswich Station*, 1963

106

102. Maggi Hambling, *Lett Dreaming*, 1975-6

List of works

All dimensions are in centimetres:
height x width (x depth)

Cedric Morris 1889-1982

1   *Self-Portrait* 1919
    Oil on board 36.8 x 26.7
    National Museums & Galleries of Wales

2   *Arthur Lett Haines* 1919
    Oil on canvas laid on board 41.9 x 31.1
    Mrs Gerald Cookson

3   *Landscape at Newlyn* 1919
    Oil on board 30.5 x 34
    Dominic Wakefield

4   *Rosa Wenslowska* 1922
    Oil on canvas 55 x 46
    Cedric Morris Estate

5   *Patisseries and a Croissant* c.1922
    Oil on canvas 35.9 x 32.7
    Tate, London

6   *Experiment in Textures* 1923
    Oil on canvas 50.1 x 59
    Tate, London

7   *Golden Auntie* 1923
    Oil on canvas 66 x 82
    Cedric Morris Estate

8   *Mary Butts* 1924
    Oil on board 68.2 x 56
    Cedric Morris Estate

9   *The Dancing Sailor* 1925
    Oil on canvas 104.1 x 104.1
    Mary Rose Tatham

10 *The Swiss Visitor* 1925
    Oil on board 81.3 x 64.7
    Chelmsford Museums (Chelmsford Borough
    Council)

11 *Paul Odo Cross* 1925
    Oil on canvas 61 x 51
    Cedric Morris Estate

12 *Still Life with Flowers* 1926
    Oil on canvas   49 x 60
    Redfern Gallery, London

13 *From a Bedroom Window at 45 Brook
    Street, W.1. 1926*
    Oil on board 91.4 x 122
    National Museums & Galleries of Wales

14 *Halcyon 1927*
    Oil on canvas 51 x 66
    Cedric Morris Estate

15 *Birds of the Air 1928*
    Oil on board 98.5 x 117
    Dominic Wakefield

16 *Llanmadoc Hill, Gower Peninsula 1928*
    Oil on canvas 65.4 x 81.2
    City and County of Swansea; Glynn Vivian Art
    Gallery Collection

17 *Nancy Morris 1929*
    Oil on canvas 50.5 x 25.4
    Cedric Morris Estate

18 *Self-Portrait c.1930*
    Oil on canvas 72.7 x 48.9
    National Portrait Gallery, London

19 *Black Tulip c.1930*
    Oil on canvas 48 x 43
    Hilary Wakefield

20 *The River Stour in Flood 1930*
    Oil on canvas 63.5 x 76.2
    Ipswich Borough Council Museums
    and Galleries

21 *Rosamund Lehmann 1932*
    Oil on canvas 52 x 39
    Sebastian Wakefield

22 *Floreat 1933*
    Oil on canvas 142.2 x 111.7
    Cyfartha Castle Museum and Art Gallery,
    Merthyr Tydfil

23 *Solva 1934*
    Oil on canvas 60.4 x 73
    Norwich Castle Museum & Art Gallery

24 *The Sisters
    (The English Upper Classes) 1935*
    Oil on canvas 76 x 63.5
    Cedric Morris Estate

25 *Miss Thomas 1935*
    Oil on canvas 45.5 x 40.5
    Cedric Morris Estate

26 *Caerharris Post Office, Dowlais 1935*
    Oil on canvas 62.2 x 76.2
    Cyfartha Castle Museum & Art Gallery,
    Merthyr Tydfil

27 *The Tips, Dowlais 1935*
Oil on canvas 64.8 x 78.8
Courtesy of Cyfartha Castle Museum &
Art Gallery, Merthyr Tydfil
(*Cardiff only*)

28 *Antonia White 1936*
Oil on canvas 49 x 42
National Portrait Gallery, London

29 *Betty Addison 1936*
Oil on canvas 61 x 51
Mary Rose Tatham

30 *David and Barbara Carr c.1940*
Oil on canvas 100.3 x 74.5
Tate, London

31 *Lucian Freud 1940*
Oil on canvas 73 x 60.2
Tate, London

32 *David Carr c.1941*
Oil no canvas 52.5 x 42
Private Collection. courtesy of the
Redfern Gallery, London

33 *Irises 1941*
Oil on canvas 90.8 x 101
Private Collection

34 *Iris Seedlings 1943*
Oil on canvas 122 x 91.7
Tate, London

35 *The Eggs 1944*
Oil on canvas 61.5 x 43.2
Tate, London

36 *Wartime Garden c.1944*
Oil on canvas 61 x 76.5
Cedric Morris Estate

37 *Flowers in a Moroccan Pot 1947*
Oil on canvas 69.2 x 43.2
Dominic Wakefield

38 *Glyn Morgan 1949*
Oil on canvas 61 x 46
Private Collection

39 *Blackbird and Flowers 1952*
Oil on canvas 65 x 109
The Jerwood Foundation

40 *Ratatouille 1954*
Oil on canvas 76 x 52
Dominic Wakefield

41 *Landscape of Shame c.1960*
Oil on canvas 75 x 100
Tate, London

42 *Chinese Quinces 1963*
Oil on canvas 90 x 121
Hilary Wakefield

43 *Millie at a Table 1966*
Oil on canvas 68.5 x 48.2
Mary Rose Tatham

44 *Flowers in a Blue Pot 1966*
Oil on canvas 72.5 x 51
Sebastian Wakefield

45 *Nasturtiums 1975*
Oil on canvas 41 x 66
Sebastian Wakefield

Works on Paper

46 *Café Scene 1921*
Pencil 35 x 24.5
Cedric Morris Estate

47 *Café Scene c.1921*
Pencil 34.5 x 24
Cedric Morris Estate

48 *Café Scene c.1921*
Pencil 35 x 24
Cedric Morris Estate

49 *Still Life 1921*
Silverpoint 25 x 19.5
Cedric Morris Estate

50 *A Roman Café 1922*
Pen and ink 31.8 x 31.2
National Museums & Galleries of Wales

51 *Fascists in Rome 1922*
Charcoal 29 x 24
Cedric Morris Estate

Arthur Lett Haines 1894-1978

52 *Portrait of Frances Hodgkins c.1919*
Charcoal 24 x 20
Dr Ronald Blythe

53 *Old Brighton Railway Station 1920*
Mixed media on paper 47 x 62.9
Private Collection

54 *Etude pour Sculpture en Bois 1920*
Black Chalk 31 x 22.9
Redfern Gallery, London

55 *Powers in Atrophe 1922*
Ink, watercolour and chalk on paper 45.9 x 43.6 Tate,
London

56 *Composition c.1922*
Mixed media on paper 46 x 63
Private collection

57 *Composition 1922*
Mixed media on paper 47 x 60
Robert Short

58 *Composition 1923*
Watercolour on paper 47 x 47
Private Collection

59 *Amusement 1922*
Gouache 35.6 x 45.7
Colchester Art Society

60 *Study of Cedric Morris 1925*
Pencil 35.6 x 24.6
National Museums & Galleries of Wales

61 *Study of Cedric Morris (reclining) 1925*
Pencil 24.6 x 35.6
National Museums & Galleries of Wales

62 *The Lion Hunt 1929*
Mixed media on paper 46.4 x 62.2
Private Collection

63 *The Escape 1931*
Mixed media on paper 47 x 61
Private Collection

64 *The Dark Horse 1934*
Watercolour and mixed media 47.8 x 62.7
Tate, London

65 *Jeunes Filles aux Fleurs 1935*
Gouache 75 x 55
Private collection
(Norwich Only)

66 *The Martyrdom of Purple Hampton 1955*
Watercolour 36.4 x 24.9
Private Collection

67 *Untitled (Composition with Flowers and
Figures) 1957*
Pencil and Watercolour on paper 35 x 25
Dr Ronald Blythe

68 *Untitled (Automatic Drawing) c.1965*
Mixed media on paper 25 x 35
Private Collection

69 *Poor Dolly 1966*
Watercolour 24.8 x 34.3
Private Collection

70 *Vue d'une Fenêtre 1967*
Watercolour 72.4 x 72.4
Redfern Gallery, London

Sculptures

71 *Dieties of the Lake (Tunisia) 1925*
Wood 17.5 x 26 x 14
Andrew and Julia Murray

72 *Mud Pie c. 1930*
Painted wood 17.5 x 14 x 13
Andrew and Julia Murray

73 *Regardant 1959*
Bone and mixed media 17.5 x 15.7 x 10.3
Private Collection

74 *Witch Fetish (Portrait of Maggi) 1962*
Bone, wood and glass 14 x 4.8 x 9.3
Private Collection

75 *Flint Desirable n.d.*
Flint and mixed media 13 x 11 x 11
Redfern Gallery, London

76 *Baked Carrot n.d.*
Carrot and mixed media 24 x 12 x 12
Redfern Gallery, London

77 *Petit Sculpture
(Jerusalem Artichoke) n.d.*
Artichoke and mixed media 12.5 x 21 x 11
Redfern Gallery, London

78 *Fetish to cause death by laughter n.d.*
Mixed media 20 x 9.5 x 9.5
Redfern Gallery, London

79 *Petit Sculpture
(Cigarette Case and Bird's skull) n.d.*
Mixed media 3.5 x 6 x 11
Redfern Gallery, London

80 *Ensemble du Banquet n.d.*
Bones and mixed media 14 x 19 x 11
Redfern Gallery, London

Frances Hodgkins 1869-1947

81 *Man with Macaw
    (Portrait of Cedric Morris)1930*
    Oil on canvas 63.5 x 53
    Towner Art Gallery, Eastbourne

82 *Flatford Mill 1930*
    Oil on canvas 72.4 x 76.2
    Tate, London

Lucy Harwood 1893-1972

83 *Still Life with Fish c.1940*
    Oil on canvas 61 x 77
    Ipswich Borough Council Museums &
    Galleries

84 *Landscape with Gulls n.d.*
    Oil on canvas 61 x 51
    Ipswich Borough Council Museums &
    Galleries

85 *The Signal   n.d.*
    Oil on canvas 51 x 61
    Private Collection

86 *Waiting for Hetty…. n.d.*
    Charcoal and crayon on paper 47 x 36
    Private Collection

87 *….and she came n.d.*
    Charcoal and crayon on paper 64.5 x 50.5
    Private Collection

David Carr 1915-68

88 *Two Women and Still Life c.1946*
    Oil on canvas 88.9 x 127
    Collection of Christopher Marshall,
    Christchurch, New Zealand

89 *Self-portrait c.1947*
    Oil on canvas 76.2 x 59.1
    Ferens Art Gallery: Hull City Museums & Art
    Gallery

90 *Man and Machine VI c.1952*
    Oil on canvas 60.6 x 51.1
    Private Collection

Lucian Freud b.1922

91 *Woman with Rejected Suitors 1939*
    Oil on canvas 60.9 x 50.8
    Private Collection

92 *Cedric Morris 1940*
    Oil on canvas 30.5 x 25.4
    National Museums & Gallerie of Wales

93 *Memory of London 1940*
    Oil on canvas 76.5 x 63.5
    Private Collection courtesy of the Timothy
     Taylor Gallery, London
    (Cardiff only)

94 *Tenby Harbour 1944*
    Crayon, charcoal and watercolour
    41.3 x 51.5
    National Museums & Galleries of Wales

Glyn Morgan b.1926

95 *Cedric Morris in his Garden c.1957*
    Oil on canvas 50.8 x 63.5
    Ipswich Borough Coucil Museums &
    Galleries

96 *The Garden at Benton End c.1960*
    Oil on board 61 x 32
    Collection of the artist

97 *Still Life with Chinese Pot 1961*
    Oil 35.6 x 45.7
    Private Collection

98 *Table of Minos VI 1971*
    Oil on canvas 51 x 51
    Collection of the artist

Maggi Hambling b.1945

99 *Rhinoceros, Ipswich Museum 1963*
    Ink on paper 48.5 x 35
    The Artist

100 *Seated Female Nude 1963*
    Etching 24.5 x 32.5
    The Artist

101 *Ipswich Station   1963*
    Etching 9 x 13
    The Artist

102 *Lett Laughing 1975-6*
    Oil on canvas 71 x 64.8
    Mrs Gerald Cookson

103 *Lett Dreaming 1975-6*

Copyright

Photographic Acknowledgements

Documentary photographs are reproduced courtesy of the Tate Archive. Figs.1,2,13 TGA 968.7.1-10; Figs.3,4,5 TGA 968.5.1; Fig.6 TGA 8317.11.7.267; Fig.10 TGA 8317.11.7.29; Fig.11 TGA 8317.1.4.90; Fig.12 TGA 8317.11.1; Fig.7 Courtesy Dr. Ronald Blythe; Figs.8, 9 Tate London.

Nos 7,9,11,15,19,36,38,44,47,48,49,50,54,58,70,98 Douglas Atfield; 16 Glynn Vivian Art Gallery; 26,27 Cyfartha Castle Museum & Art Gallery; 53,63, 64, 66,69,73,74 Hugh Kelly;5,6,30,31,34,35,41,58,64,82 Tate London; 1,13,92,94 National Museums and Galleries of Wales; 20,83,84,95 Ipswich Borough Council Museums and Galleries; 23 Norwich Castle Museum & Art Gallery; 18,28 National Portrait Gallery, London; 39 The Jerwood Foundation; 57,85,90 GGS Photographics; 82 Towner Art Gallery, Eastbourne; 89 Ferens Art Gallery, Hull City Museums and Galleries / Bridgeman Art Library; 91 Bridgeman Art Library; 93 Courtesy Timothy Taylor Gallery, London; 99,100,101 Miki Slingsby; 103 Chelmsford Museums (Chelmsford Borough Council).